W9-BFZ-453

JO VERSO'S
CROSS STITCH YEAR

1001 MOTIFS TO CELEBRATE
THE EVENTS OF THE SEASONS

Spring

birds are nesting

new life's begun

snowdrops nodding

now Spring has sprung

Summer

fruit and flowers

the skies are clear

bees are buzzing

Summer is here

Autumn

warm apple pies

at harvest time

with falling leaves

make Autumn's rhyme

Winter

cold wind and snow

make toes go numb

holly and ivy

mean Winter's come

JO VERSO'S
CROSS STITCH
YEAR

1001 MOTIFS TO CELEBRATE
THE EVENTS OF THE SEASONS

January freezes, so February sneezes,
March blows, then April grows,
May swells buds, ere June brings floods,
It boils in July and in August we fry,
September mists swirl, October leaves curl,
November is drear,
But Yule brings good cheer.

DAVID & CHARLES

To Judy, Gordon and Chris Gore,
whose friendship has sustained me through more than one year.

(Above) The October garland mounted in a circular wooden bowl lid

(Half-title page) A gardener's card using figures from the Garden in Spring (page 26)

(Title page) The four seasonal Band Samplers

A DAVID & CHARLES BOOK

First published in the UK in 1998

Text and designs Copyright © Jo Verso 1998
Photography and layout Copyright © David & Charles 1998

Jo Verso has asserted her right to be identified as author of this work
in accordance with the Copyright, Designs and Patents Act, 1988.

The designs in this book are copyright and must not be stitched for resale.

All rights reserved. No part of this publication may be reproduced,
stored in a retrieval system, or transmitted, in any form or by any means,
electronic or mechanical, by photocopying, recording or otherwise,
without prior permission in writing from the publisher.

A catalogue record for this book is available from the British Library.

ISBN 0 7153 0477 1

Photography by David Johnson
Styling by Kit Johnson
Book design and diagrams by Ethan Danielson
and printed in Great Britain by Butler &Tanner Ltd, Frome, Somerset
for David & Charles
Brunel House   Newton Abbot   Devon

 # CONTENTS

When I sat down in 1986 to write my first book, *Picture It in Cross Stitch*, little did I realise what a huge response it would generate. Soon after publication it became obvious that, just like me, there were many stitchers who wanted to stitch a personal record of their lives. It appeared that my book gave them the tools to achieve it without the terror of having to design from scratch. I was amazed and delighted to discover that with my designs of the people, animals, and items that we encounter in daily life many unique samplers were created, giving enormous pleasure to the stitchers and possibly providing a source of interest for future generations.

In response to demand I wrote the follow-up book, *World of Cross Stitch*, which included more designs of domestic life and which went further afield to cater for those who travel or who have friends and relatives abroad. Since then I have met many stitchers who tell me that they require even more designs to include in their samplers. In stitching magazines I have read with interest the requests for elusive designs and so this book has been written in response to these continuing demands and will, I hope, provide even more grist for your mills.

My theme for the designs in this book is the seasons throughout the year, the high days and holidays and the differing activities that take place with the changing months. Living in England as I do, I enjoy the dramatic changes that each season brings, the opportunities that each offers and the demands that each makes on our way of life. Included are flora and fauna, zodiac signs, birthday cards, feast days and the activities associated with each passing month and season.

FLORAL GARLANDS SAMPLER
(pictured opposite)
Finished size: 9¹/2 x 12¹/2in (24 x 32cm).
Worked on cream 27 count Zweigart Linda. To stitch this sampler work the monthly floral garlands, which are charted throughout the book, lining them up side by side and in rows. As a finishing touch, stitch a seasonal brass charm in the centre of each floral garland. To prevent tarnishing, clean brass charms with alcohol and seal them with a thin coat of clear varnish before applying them to embroidery. If preferred, stitch a date or name in the central space.

As you look through the book you may recognise friends or relatives, the activities in which they take part or events that are important in your own life. Many designs can be stitched off the page and colour keys have been provided wherever practical, but my main hope is that you will take designs which have a personal meaning for you and put them together to make your own samplers, pictures, cards or gifts, as you have been doing so successfully with the other two books.

I hope that you will look further than at what is actually on the page and see the possibilities that each design can offer. For example, you may not want to stitch the design for Shrove Tuesday, it may not be an important date in your calendar, but do you know a hopeless cook with a sense of humour? By changing the lettering you can make a personal card for her and alphabets are included throughout the book to assist you. I do not play rugby myself, but as the current saying goes, I know a man who does, and he would be tickled pink to be immortalised in cross stitch. Small designs can be extracted from large ones, for example you may not want to stitch the Chinese New Year design, but perhaps you know an animal lover and could stitch one of the animals either onto a sampler, or as a small card. The photographs show how versatile the designs can be and will hopefully spark off your own ideas for projects. Many of you are old hands at this, but for those who aren't, step-by-step instructions are offered to take the terror out of designing.

If you need an extra design to complete your sampler, which is not to be found in this book, you could try looking in my five other books, which might contain the very design you need. Perhaps you need to adapt a figure to more closely resemble the person you want to depict; the chances are that you will find the hairstyle, clothing or accessories that complete the picture. My style is consistent throughout my work, so designs from previous books can be worked alongside those offered here.

I have included instructions for stitching a flawless result and wherever possible I have listed suppliers to enable you to acquire the necessary items to produce a similar result to the one shown. This is accurate at the time of going to print, but not all businesses survive so in years to come you may have to improvise.

Over the years many of you have been kind enough to write to me sending photographs of your work and showing me the ingenious and unique pieces of stitching that you have produced using my designs. I have kept every letter and all the photographs are collected together in a large album, which I treasure. I hope very much that with the help of this book you too will be able to design with ease and stitch with pleasure all year round.

FABRICS

You will need either evenweave or Aida fabric to stitch the designs in this book.

EVENWEAVE FABRIC

Evenweave fabric is woven with single threads and is available in a variety of colours and thread counts, a thread count being the number of threads there are to 1in (2.5cm). The smaller the number of threads, the larger the weave is and the larger the cross stitches worked on it will be. Conversely, the higher the number of threads to 1in (2.5cm), the finer the fabric and the smaller the cross stitches will be. Cross stitches are worked over two threads of the fabric (see Fig 4 page 10). Designs containing three-quarter cross stitches are best worked on evenweave fabric where a central hole will be available to accommodate the quarter stitch (see Fig 8 page 11).

AIDA FABRIC

Aida fabric is available in a variety of colours and thread counts. It is woven to form blocks of threads between each hole and the cross stitch is worked over one block (see Fig 5 page 10).

CHOOSING FABRIC

Choose a fabric which does not strain your eyesight; stitching is supposed to be a pleasure not a struggle. When using a coarser fabric than the one recommended, the result will be the same but larger, so check that the finished work will fit the mount that you intend to use. To do this, count the number of squares on your design both horizontally and vertically. Divide these numbers by the number of stitches produced per inch (2.5cm) of your chosen fabric and you will know the size of the finished, stitched design. For example, if a chart measuring 100 squares by 50 squares is worked on a fabric which produces 10 cross stitches to 1in (2.5cm) the finished embroidery will measure 10in (25cm) by 5in (12.5cm).

Buy or cut a piece of fabric large enough to accommodate your finished design, remembering to leave a good margin all round for turnings when mounting or framing. Oversew the edges of the fabric to prevent fraying and iron out any stubborn creases in the fabric before you start to stitch.

Find the centre of the fabric by folding it in four and mark temporarily with a pin. If the central stitch of the design is worked at this point, the design will be correctly centred on the fabric. Mount the fabric into an embroidery hoop large enough to accommodate the whole design

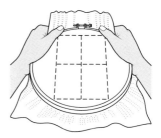

Fig 1 Fabric mounted into a hoop

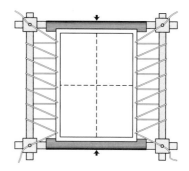

Fig 2 Fabric mounted into a frame

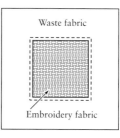

Fig 3 Adding waste fabric

(Fig 1), or mount it into a suitably sized embroidery frame (Fig 2). This will ensure that your fabric is stretched taut and will enable you to keep an even tension throughout your stitching. Small pieces of fabric can be mounted into hoops or frames if extra waste fabric is stitched to them first. Lay your embroidery fabric centrally on a piece of waste cotton fabric (I use pieces of worn-out pillowcases). Stitch the two pieces of fabric together around the edges of the embroidery fabric and cut away the cotton fabric on the reverse exposing the back of the embroidery fabric (Fig 3). Mount the fabric into a hoop or onto a frame. When work is complete cut away the waste fabric.

(Opposite) The Four Garden Samplers

EMBROIDERY SCISSORS

You will need sharp, fine-pointed embroidery scissors to cut thread and to trim ends of thread on the back of the work. Use dressmaking scissors to cut fabric and ensure that your embroidery scissors are used solely to cut embroidery thread. Blunt scissors will chew the thread and leave untidy tufts on the back of the work that will show through and spoil the appearance of the work when it is mounted.

NEEDLES

You will need a blunt tapestry needle which will slip easily through the holes in your fabric without piercing or splitting the threads. The needle should be sufficiently fine to slip through the holes without enlarging or distorting them. Finer needles have a higher number on the packet (26); thicker needles have a lower number (18). A size 26 was used for the majority of the work in this book. Stitchers who find that that the plating on the needle wears off as they stitch, leaving them with a rough needle, can solve the problem by using gold-plated needles.

THREADS

All the designs in this book were worked with stranded cottons. Both DMC and Anchor stranded cottons are readily available in a multitude of colours.

Cut a length of stranded cotton from the skein and separate the required number of threads. Do not be tempted to cut very long lengths as the thread will tangle and knot. Use sufficient strands to give good coverage of the fabric. On fabrics that produce 13–18 cross stitches to 1in (2.5cm) use two strands for cross stitch; coarser fabrics may require more strands and finer fabrics may require less. Work a few stitches to check coverage and adjust the number of strands to suit the fabric. Backstitch and French knots are generally worked with one strand.

STITCHES
FULL CROSS STITCH

One completely filled square on your chart indicates the use of one full cross stitch on your fabric. When working on evenweave fabric, work the full cross stitch over two threads (Fig 4). When working on Aida fabric work the full cross stitch over one block (Fig 5). When working rows of full cross stitches, bring the needle out at the left-hand side of the row and work a row of half crosses. Return, making the complete crosses, working from right to left and using the same holes as before (Fig 6). All stitches 'hold hands', sharing holes with their neighbours, unless they are single stitches worked on their own. Ensure that all top stitches are lying in the same direction to give a uniform appearance to your work. Do not allow

twists to develop on the thread as this will lead to poor coverage of the fabric. Untwist the thread regularly by allowing the needle to dangle, or use a technique called railroading when you are working with two strands of thread in the needle. Before inserting your needle into the hole in the fabric, separate the two strands of cotton coming from the previous hole and pass the needle between the two strands as it enters the next hole. This serves to separate the strands, remove any twists from them and ensure that they lie neatly side by side (Fig 7).

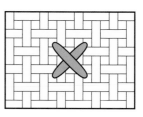

Fig 4 A full cross stitch worked over two threads on evenweave fabric

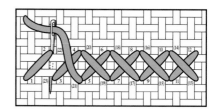

Fig 5 A full cross stitch worked over one block on Aida fabric

Fig 6 Working a line of full cross stitches

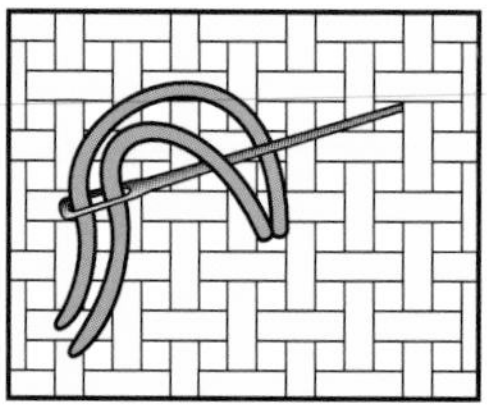

Fig 7 Railroading

THREE-QUARTER CROSS STITCH

This will be indicated on your chart by a right-angled triangle. The first half of the cross stitch is formed in the usual way but the second 'quarter' stitch is brought over the half cross and down into the central hole (Fig 8). The rule of having the top stitches always lying in the same direction is thus sometimes broken, but by bringing the 'quarter' stitch over the top, the longer bottom stitch is anchored down firmly giving a neater effect. Where the chart indicates two three-quarter stitches occupying the space of one full cross stitch, these are worked back to back, sharing the same central hole (Fig 9).

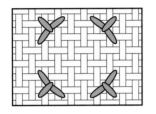

Fig 8 Four examples of three-quarter cross stitch worked on evenweave fabric

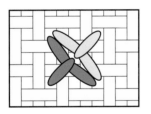

Fig 9 Two three-quarter cross stitches worked back to back, occupying the space of one full cross stitch

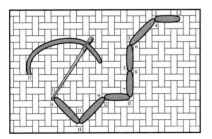

Fig 10 Backstitch

BACKSTITCH

The use of backstitch is indicated on your chart by a solid line. When all the full and three-quarter cross stitches have been worked, backstitch can be worked around or over them to add detail and definition. It can also be used to work lettering. Backstitch is worked either over two threads or one, depending on the direction indicated on the chart.

With reference to Fig 10, bring the needle out at 1 and in again at 2. Bring it out again at 3 and in again at 4. Continue this sequence in the direction indicated by your chart. Where the chart shows a backstitch bisecting a full cross stitch, take the thread over the top of the cross stitch (Fig 11).

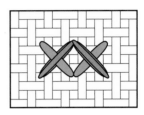

Fig 11 Backstitch worked over a cross stitch

FRENCH KNOTS

The use of this stitch will be indicated on your chart by a dot or a knot symbol. To sew a French knot bring your needle out one thread to the right of where you want the knot to lie. Lay the embroidery on a table or on your knee so that both your hands are free. Holding the thread between finger and thumb in your left hand and the needle in your right, twist the thread twice around the needle in a counter-clockwise direction. Insert the needle back into the fabric, one thread to the left (Fig 12). Gently tighten, but not overtighten, the twists around the needle. Lift the embroidery in your left hand, holding the thread coming from the needle firmly against the fabric. Very gently and slowly pull the needle through to the back without allowing the twists to unravel. Pull the last 1in (2.5cm) of thread through extra carefully to form a perfect, circular French knot.

Do not be tempted to work French knots with more than two or three twists. If a bigger knot is required, use more strands of thread or a thicker needle. If more twists are used the knot will not be circular.

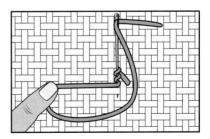

Fig 12 Working a French knot

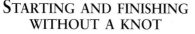
STARTING AND FINISHING WITHOUT A KNOT

Knots on the back of embroidery are to be avoided as they form lumps that will distort the work when it is mounted.

STARTING A NEW THREAD AGAINST EXISTING STITCHES

Where a new colour butts up against existing stitches, the new thread can be run through the back of two or three of the stitches already worked. Make a small backstitch to secure it and bring the thread to the right side to start work.

STARTING A NEW THREAD IN BARE FABRIC

Where there are no existing stitches onto which new thread can be anchored, another technique is needed. With reference to Fig 13a, insert the needle at A, leaving a short tail on the front of the work. Bring the needle out at B where the stitching is to start. Stitch in the direction of A, catching the thread at the back as you sew (Fig 13b). After a few stitches the thread will be secure and the loose end can be trimmed off neatly on the back of the work.

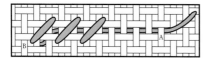

Fig 13a Starting without the use of a knot (right side of fabric)

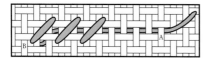

Fig 13b Starting without the use of a knot (wrong side of fabric)

LOOP STARTING METHOD

When working with two strands in the needle use the loop starting method. Cut a length of stranded cotton and separate one strand from the length. Double it to give two strands. Thread the two ends through the eye of the needle to form a loop that hangs from the needle. Bring the needle to the surface of the fabric at the starting

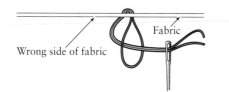

Fig 14 The loop starting method

point, leaving the loop on the back of the work. Take the needle to the back of the work to make the first half of the cross stitch and thread the needle through the loop (Fig 14). Tighten the thread for a neat, knotless start.

A KNOTLESS FINISH

A knotless finish can be worked as follows. On the back of the fabric, thread the needle through the back of the last three stitches worked, taking care not to distort them. Return, jumping over one stitch and threading the needle through the back of two stitches. Trim the thread neatly, close to the stitching, using sharp embroidery scissors (Fig 15).

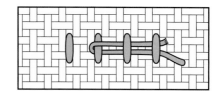

Fig 15 Finishing without the use of a knot (wrong side of fabric)

HINTS AND TIPS

• Do not choose colours in poor light or at night: you could get an unpleasant surprise the next morning.
• Before starting to stitch, lay your threads on your chosen fabric to check that the background colour of the fabric tones well with the colour of the threads.
• Press any stubborn creases out of your fabric before you start to stitch.
• Avoid soiling your work by always washing your hands before stitching and by keeping the work covered when you are not stitching.
• Avoid carrying thread across the back of bare fabric. A ghostly trail will be visible when the work is mounted. It is, however, acceptable to run thread for short distances from one area to another through the back of existing stitches, taking care not to distort them.
• Trim off ends neatly on the back of the work. Even the smallest tuft can be visible and will spoil the appearance of your work when it is mounted.
• Count your stitches carefully as you proceed and check your work regularly against the chart. Having to unpick and rework is very disheartening.
• Remove twists from your thread as you work or use the railroading technique to get the best coverage of the fabric.
• To press your work with an iron, lay it face down on a thick, soft, white, terry towel. Avoid pressing on a hard surface which will flatten the stitches.
• Work in a strong light, either by a window during daylight or under a lamp at night.

STITCHING THE PROJECTS

To enable you to achieve results identical to the photographed samples of the stitch-off-the-page designs in this book, I have listed the fabrics that were used. Sizes are approximate and given to the nearest 1/4in (0.5cm), but remember that if a fabric with a different thread count is used the end result will not be the same size.

CHINESE NEW YEAR
(charted on page 123)
Finished size: 5 x 6in (13 x 15.5cm). Worked on white 27 count Zweigart Linda.

The designs in this book offer the possibility for you to put together your own very personal view of the year in a cross stitch sampler. To many people the prospect of designing is fraught with difficulty, but by following a few simple suggestions excellent results can be achieved.

1 Go through the book and make a list of what you would like to include in your sampler. Copy out each design on the list onto graph paper. Colour in each design using coloured crayons. Find a suitable alphabet and draw out the name of each month and any other words which you require. You may want to incorporate all important birthdays and anniversaries as I have done, if so copy these out as well. Using paper-cutting scissors to avoid blunting your embroidery scissors, cut out each design and block of lettering leaving one clear square all the way round (Fig 16). As you work, keep the design slips safely in an envelope to prevent them straying and ending up in the vacuum cleaner or the dog.

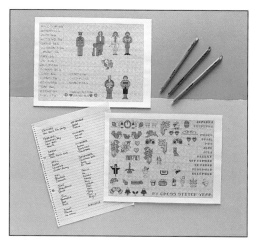

Listing, then copying designs onto graph paper

2 Take a large sheet of matching graph paper, large enough to contain the whole design. Large sheets of graph paper can be purchased from art and craft or stationery shops, or be made by sticking small sheets together carefully. Lay all your design slips onto this background sheet and you are ready to start building up your design. A common mistake is to start drawing enthusiastically straight onto the background sheet. Inevitably you will change your mind many times, which means liberal use of the eraser and considerable irritation, as things have to be re-drawn over and over again. Using my method you can try many different arrangements of the design material without having to re-draw once.

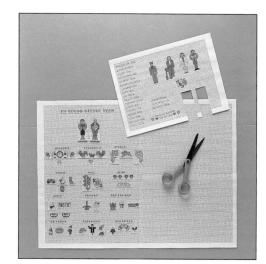

Cutting out, then arranging designs on a background sheet

3 Shuffle the slips around on the background sheet until you achieve a pleasing and balanced design. You may have to copy out more designs to fill gaps, or reject some of your first ideas in favour of others. Try to avoid having a design facing out of the picture. Wherever possible

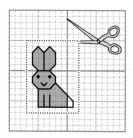

*Fig 16 Cut out your drawings,
leaving one clear square all round*

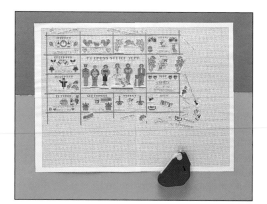

*Re-arranging to get a better result, then
sticking designs to the background sheet*

reverse the design so that the eye is drawn towards the centre. To do this, hold a small hand mirror next to the design and copy out the reflection.

I chose an arrangement which left a large gap in the centre which I filled with family members and pets, but you might choose to fill the centre of your design with your house or a larger design of the most important event in your cross stitch year. I organised the designs for each month into 'boxes' but if you prefer a freer approach, dispense with the boxes and then the months can be positioned anywhere you like. My sampler is landscape-shaped, but you may prefer to have a portrait-shaped sampler with six rows of two months, omitting the central space, or even a circular sampler arranged like a clock face. If one event during the year is of particular importance to you, place it in the centre and surround it with the other months; the possibilities are endless and with this system you can try them all out before you commit yourself.

Decide whether your design needs a border or a simple line to contain it. If you wish to add a border, copy it out onto strips of graph paper and fit it around the design. Borders rarely turn corners just where you want them to, so some rearrangement of the design material in the centre may be needed at this stage.

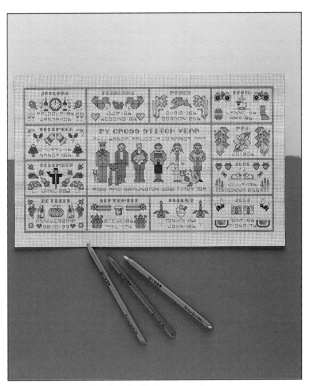

The finished design, redrawn to create a pattern for stitching

My alternative designs for a cross stitch sampler of the events of the year show how wide the range of possibilities are – have fun designing your own

4 When you are satisfied with your arrangement of all the slips, stick them to the background sheet of graph paper using adhesive. A non-permanent adhesive, such as Pelikan Rollfix or Spray Mount, allows you to reposition the slips several times. When positioning, take care to align the squares on the slips with the squares on the background sheet.

5 Pin up your design in a room where you will see it frequently: if anything needs to be changed or moved it will soon become obvious. It is easier to make the required changes at this stage rather than when stitching is in progress. When you are satisfied with your design draw it out again onto another large sheet of graph paper which will serve as a pattern for stitching. It is tempting to skip this stage, but the non-permanent glue might allow slips to come adrift and get lost during stitching.

This five-step process can be used not only for designing samplers but also for any other project where you choose to combine different designs. The Hallowe'en card (see photograph on page 86) was devised in this way from the design material on page 91. Those stitchers fortunate enough to have access to a cross stitch computer programme will be able to take many short cuts but the principles remain the same.

YOUR QUESTIONS ANSWERED

How can I change a figure to look more like the person I want to depict?

a) Copy out the figure closest to your needs.

b) Erase those features you do not want.

c) Draw in the new details which can be taken from another figure.

d) Using coloured pencils, colour in your new figure (Fig 17).

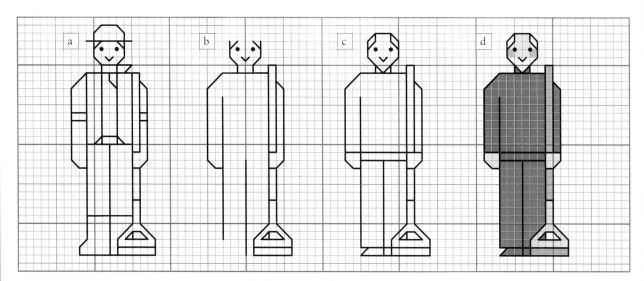

Fig 17 How to change a figure

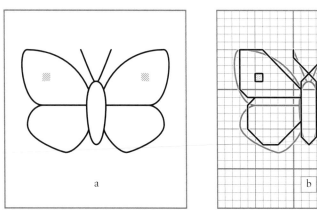
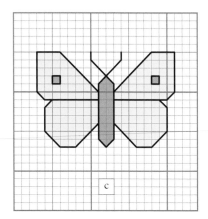

Fig 18 Squaring-up a design – stages in copying and transferring an illustration onto graph paper

My Cross Stitch Year – the finished embroidery

What do I do if I want to include an item which does not appear in your books for me to copy?

If you cannot draw the item yourself then tracing paper will come to the rescue. Find an illustration of the item: useful sources can be catalogues, photographs, postcards or your local library where you will find that children's books are invaluable for simple line drawings. Trace the illustration onto tracing paper and transfer it to graph paper, or trace directly onto tracing graph paper. Square up the design to make a pattern (Fig 18 left). Draw close to the original lines but remember that a cross stitch forms a square shape when sewn (Fig 19 overleaf), a three-quarter stitch forms a right-angled triangle (Fig 20) but no other fraction of a square is stitchable so ensure that your design contains only a combination of these shapes. Erase the original lines to reveal your new pattern.

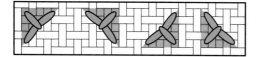

Fig 19 A full cross stitch forms
a square shape when sewn

Fig 20 A three-quarter cross stitch forms
a right-angled triangle when sewn

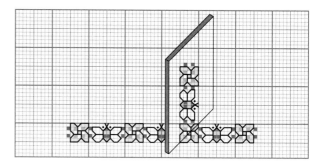

Fig 21 Using a hand mirror to invent a corner

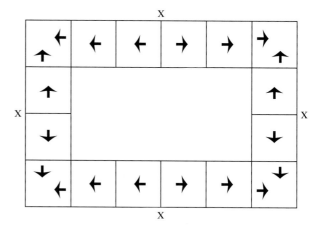

Fig 22 Pattern repeats slope in the direction
of the arrows, and reversal points at X
give the border four similar corners

*How do I enlarge or reduce an illustration that
I want to chart?*
If the illustration you wish to use is the wrong size to
match the rest of your design, you will need access to a
modern photocopier. These machines can enlarge or
reduce an illustration at minimal cost and can be found at
your local high street printing shop.

How do I make a pattern of my house or a building?
Houses and buildings consist mostly of straight lines. If
confident, you can draw your house directly onto graph
paper, taking care to get the proportions right. Start with
the smallest detail that you want to record, perhaps the
door-knocker or a small window. Build the house up
around this. Check the size and spacing of the doors and
windows, then add the outer walls, ground line and roof.
Finally add any details that will make it look like home, a
window box perhaps, or your cat at the front window.
If this seems too daunting then tracing graph paper makes
the job easier if it is placed over a sketch or photograph
of the house. If the photograph is too small or too large,
take a tracing of it and have it enlarged or reduced on a
photocopier to the desired size.

*How do I get a band to turn a corner to make a border
for my sampler?*
If there is a band which you would like to use to make a
continuous border you will have to invent a corner with
the use of a small hand mirror. Place the mirror on the
band at an angle of 45 degrees and move it along the
band until a pleasing corner is reflected in the mirror (Fig
21). Copy this reflection onto graph paper. Where a pattern repeat slopes in one direction it may be desirable to
break the run in the centre of each side and reverse the
pattern at this point to ensure four similar corners (Fig
22). This was the method used when designing the border
on page 37 (Fig 23).

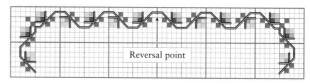

Fig 23 Reversal point

CALENDAR OF FEAST DAYS
(pictured opposite)
Finished size: 7^{1}/$_{2}$ x 10^{3}/$_{4}$in (19 x 27.5cm).
Worked on cream 27 count Zweigart Linda.
This calendar was stitched from the feast
day designs charted in each month and the
lettering was added using the alphabet
charts on pages 30 and 36. For instructions
on making the bible marker see page 125.

If the oak's before the ash
Then you'll only get a splash
But if the ash 🐛🐛🐛
🦋 🦋 precedes the oak
Then you may expect a soak.

APPLE BLOSSOM · BLUEBELLS · CATKINS · DAFFS · EGGS
A B C D E F
FROGSPAWN · GREENFINCH · HARE · IRIS · JONQUIL · KITE · LAMB
G H I J K L M
MAGNOLIA · NEST · OWLET · PRIMROSE · QUAIL · RABBIT · SNOWDROP
N O P Q R S T
TULIP · UMBRELLA · VIOLET · WINDMILL · VALENTINE KISSES
U V W X Y Z
YELLOW PANSIES AND ZANDER FOR A SPRINGTIME A B C

April

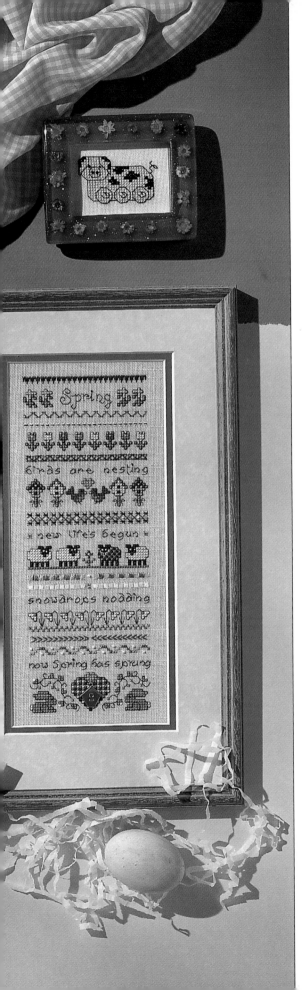

SPRING

*March winds and April showers
Bring forth May flowers.*

*Stitch-off-the-page designs
to celebrate the season of spring.*

SPRING ALPHABET
(charted on pages 22–23)
Finished size: 9³/4 x 7¹/4in (25 x 18.5cm).
Worked on cream 27 count Zweigart
Linda. Letters from the alphabet can be
extracted to stitch initials, names or events
through the season.

SPRING BAND SAMPLER
(charted on page 24)
Finished size: 3¹/2 x 9¹/2in (9 x 24cm).
Worked on 28 count Country Style
Evenweave (NJ449.26).
When work is complete, stitch a seasonal
brass charm onto the heart at the bottom of
the design. To prevent tarnishing, clean
brass charms with alcohol and seal them
with a thin coat of clear varnish before
applying them to embroidery. Frame the
sampler or hang it from bell-pull ends to
make a small hanging.

SPRING WEATHER FOLKLORE
(charted on page 25)
Finished size: 5¹/2 x 3³/4in (14 x 9.5cm).
Worked on cream 14 count Zweigart Aida.

THE GARDEN IN SPRING
(charted on page 26, photographed on page 27)
Finished size: 6 x 6³/4in (15 x 17cm).
Worked on 28 count Country Style
Evenweave (NJ449.20).

*Spring Alphabet, Spring Band Sampler and Spring Weather
Folklore, plus other items from this season. Each month also
has a photograph showing a variety of completed pieces to
give you some ideas on how the charts may be used*

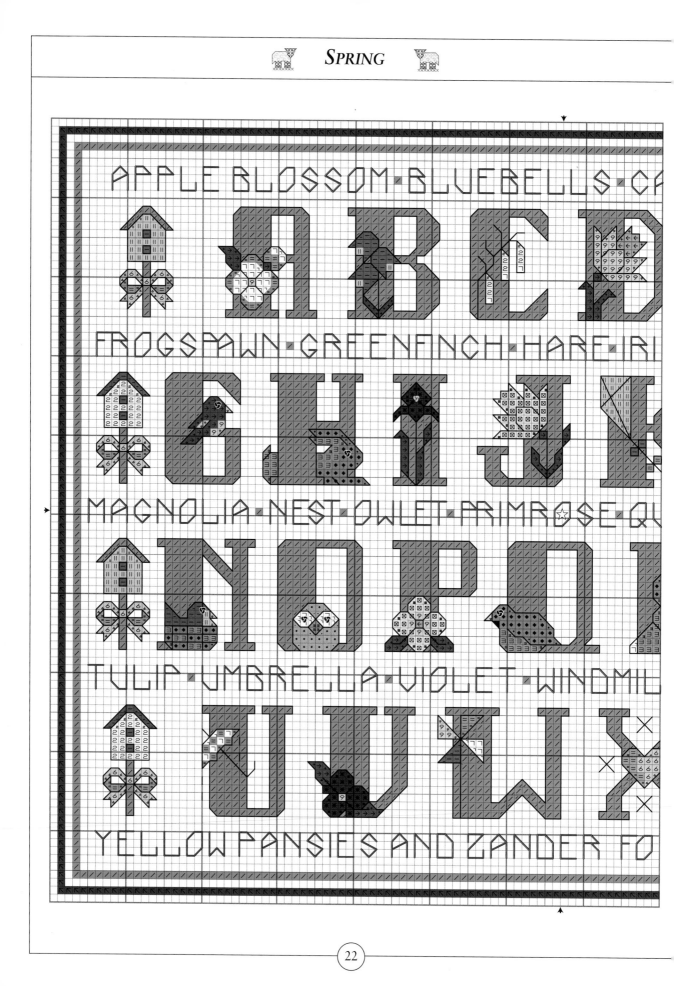

APPLE BLOSSOM · BLUEBELLS · C

A B C D

FROGSPAWN · GREENFINCH · HARE · IRI

G H I J K

MAGNOLIA · NEST · OWLET · PRIMROSE · Q

N O P Q

TULIP · UMBRELLA · VIOLET · WINDMIL

U V W X

YELLOW PANSIES AND ZANDER FO

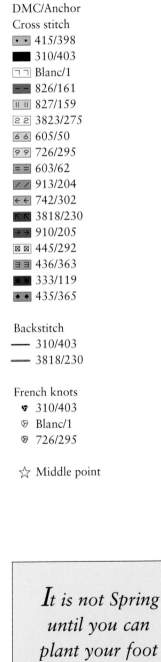

SPRING ALPHABET

Colour Key

DMC/Anchor
Cross stitch

- 415/398
- 310/403
- Blanc/1
- 826/161
- 827/159
- 3823/275
- 605/50
- 726/295
- 603/62
- 913/204
- 742/302
- 3818/230
- 910/205
- 445/292
- 436/363
- 333/119
- 435/365

Backstitch

— 310/403
— 3818/230

French knots

- 310/403
- Blanc/1
- 726/295

☆ Middle point

*It is not Spring
until you can
plant your foot
on twelve daisies.*

SPRING BAND SAMPLER

Key to Stitches

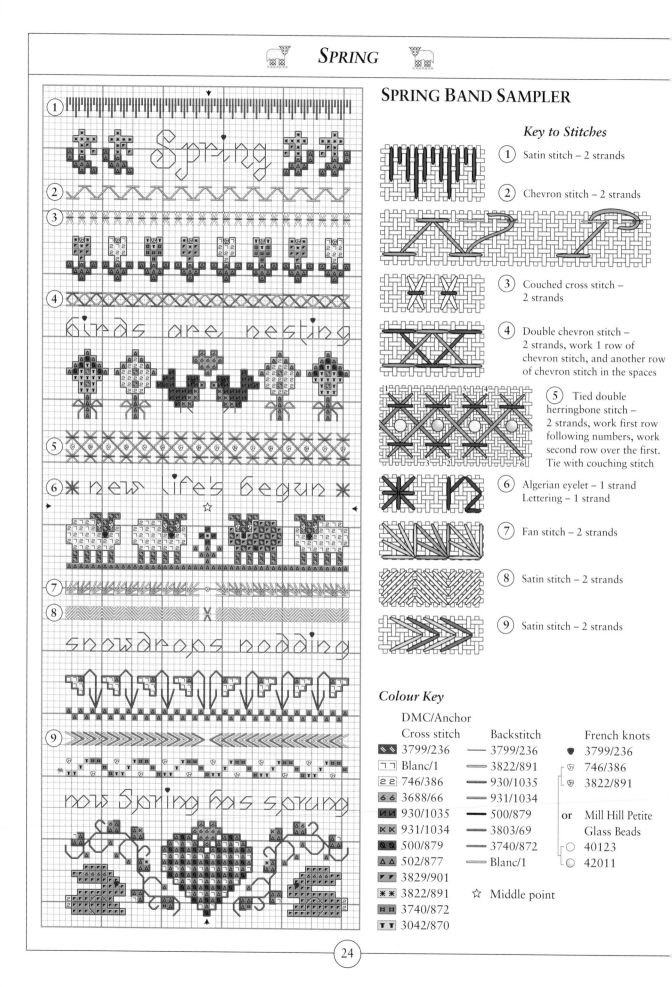

1. Satin stitch – 2 strands

2. Chevron stitch – 2 strands

3. Couched cross stitch – 2 strands

4. Double chevron stitch – 2 strands, work 1 row of chevron stitch, and another row of chevron stitch in the spaces

5. Tied double herringbone stitch – 2 strands, work first row following numbers, work second row over the first. Tie with couching stitch

6. Algerian eyelet – 1 strand
   Lettering – 1 strand

7. Fan stitch – 2 strands

8. Satin stitch – 2 strands

9. Satin stitch – 2 strands

Colour Key

DMC/Anchor

Cross stitch	Backstitch	French knots
3799/236	—— 3799/236	3799/236
Blanc/1	—— 3822/891	746/386
746/386	—— 930/1035	3822/891
3688/66	—— 931/1034	
930/1035	—— 500/879	**or** Mill Hill Petite
931/1034	—— 3803/69	Glass Beads
500/879	—— 3740/872	40123
502/877	—— Blanc/1	42011
3829/901		
3822/891	☆ Middle point	
3740/872		
3042/870		

Birds are nesting

new life's begun

snowdrops nodding

now Spring has sprung

> *I*f the oak's before the ash
> *T*hen you'll only get a splash
> *B*ut if the ash precedes the oak
> *T*hen you may expect a soak.

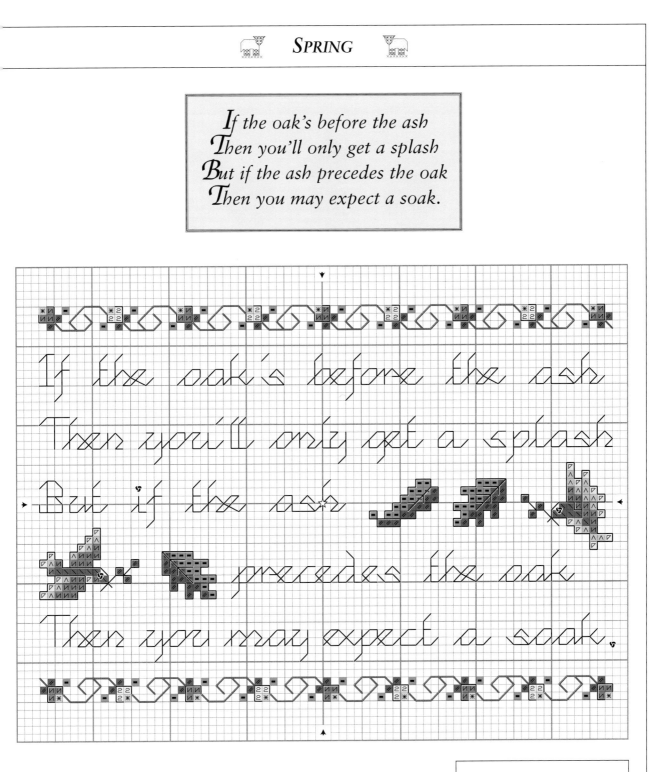

SPRING WEATHER FOLKLORE

Colour Key

DMC/Anchor

Cross stitch

2 2	745/386	И И 334/977	⁄ ⁄ 700/239	
▽ ▽	775/975	∧ ∧ 3325/976	✳ ✳ 725/306	
＼ ＼	322/978	▬ ▬ 703/238		

Backstitch
— 310/403
— 700/239
☆ Middle point

French knots
❦ 310/403

*F*or every fog
in March
*T*here'll be a
frost in May.

THE GARDEN IN SPRING

Colour Key

DMC/Anchor
Cross stitch

• • 414/235	⌐⌐ 353/6	⊐⊐ 726/295
⟍⟍ 415/398	‖‖ 352/9	88 310/403
⊤⊤ 701/227	22 798/131	99 699/923
– – 738/361	33 433/371	•⁖ 720/324
	44 321/9046	⊨⊨ 301/349
	55 Blanc/1	:::: 552/99
		⟩⟩ 938/381
		++ 604/55
		⟋⟋ 703/225
		⊠⊠ 746/386

Backstitch

— 310/403
— 415/398
— 703/225
— 699/923
═ Blanc/1

French knots

🌰 798/131
🌀 310/403
⊚ 746/386

☆ Middle point

MARCH

March comes in like a lion and goes out like a lamb.

Winter pansies form a garland for a March birthday card and beneath it are other seasonal flowers to add a touch of spring to your stitching.

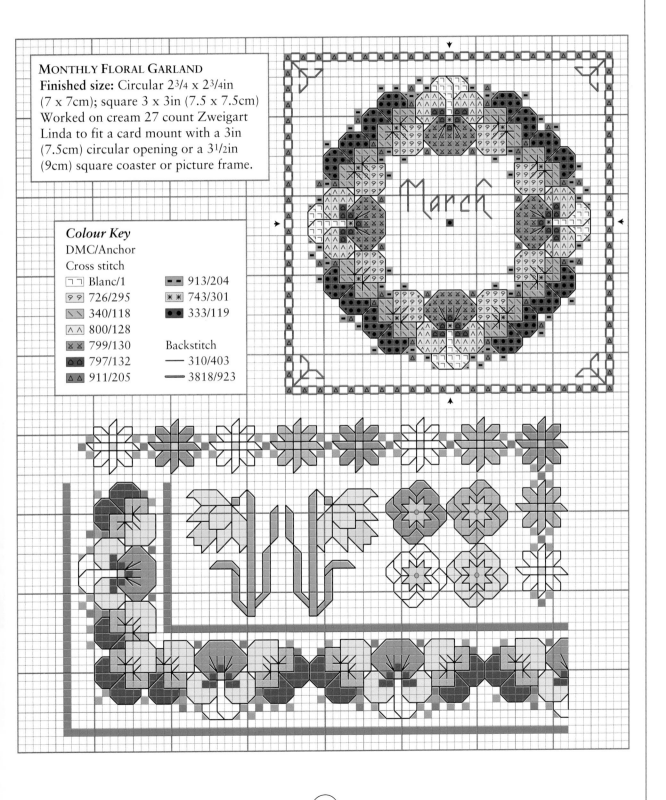

MONTHLY FLORAL GARLAND

Finished size: Circular 2³/4 x 2³/4in (7 x 7cm); square 3 x 3in (7.5 x 7.5cm) Worked on cream 27 count Zweigart Linda to fit a card mount with a 3in (7.5cm) circular opening or a 3¹/2in (9cm) square coaster or picture frame.

Colour Key

DMC/Anchor

Cross stitch

⊓⊓	Blanc/1	▬▬	913/204
9 9	726/295	✳✳	743/301
\ \	340/118	●●	333/119
∧∧	800/128		
✕✕	799/130		Backstitch
△△	797/132	——	310/403
△△	911/205	══	3818/923

A zodiac design, spring flowers and motifs for notable dates in March, such as the national saints' days.

Pisces (19th February – 20th March)

25th March: Feast Day – The Annunciation

17th March: St Patrick's Day

1st March: St David's Day

*The mad March hare appears in the countryside, whilst
dogs of every breed are groomed for their moment of glory at Crufts,
the most famous dog show in the world. Other mutts can only dream.*

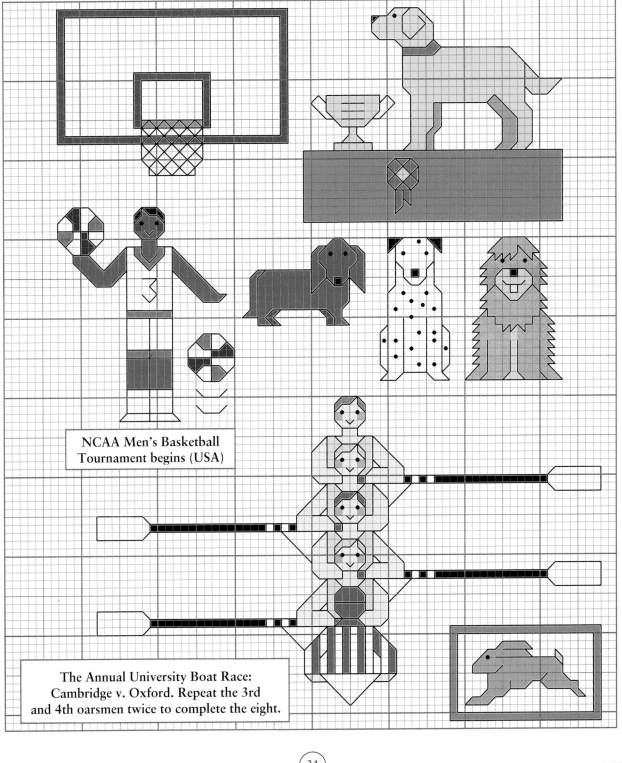

NCAA Men's Basketball
Tournament begins (USA)

The Annual University Boat Race:
Cambridge v. Oxford. Repeat the 3rd
and 4th oarsmen twice to complete the eight.

In spring Mother Nature is busy producing the next
generation. These newborn animals with their mothers
make ideal motifs to be stitched as Mother's Day cards.

This is a busy time of year in the vegetable garden when digging must be done and seeds must be sown. To ensure a bumper crop, the wise gardener will heed this advice handed down over generations.

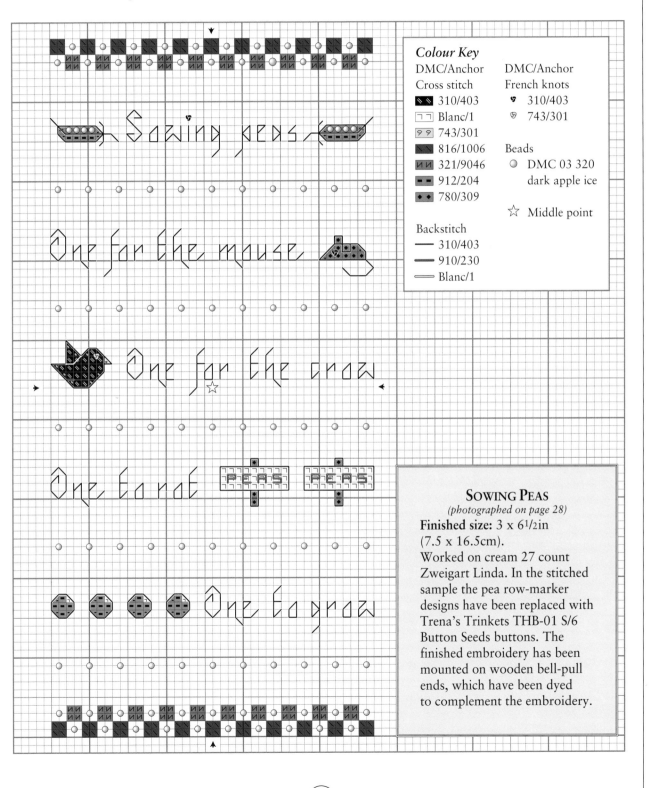

Colour Key

DMC/Anchor	
Cross stitch	
■ 310/403	
⊓ Blanc/1	
9 743/301	
816/1006	
⋈ 321/9046	
▬ 912/204	
◆ 780/309	

Backstitch
— 310/403
— 910/230
═ Blanc/1

DMC/Anchor
French knots
❤ 310/403
♥ 743/301

Beads
○ DMC 03 320
dark apple ice

☆ Middle point

SOWING PEAS
(photographed on page 28)
Finished size: 3 x 6½in
(7.5 x 16.5cm).
Worked on cream 27 count
Zweigart Linda. In the stitched
sample the pea row-marker
designs have been replaced with
Trena's Trinkets THB-01 S/6
Button Seeds buttons. The
finished embroidery has been
mounted on wooden bell-pull
ends, which have been dyed
to complement the embroidery.

APRIL

*The cuckoo comes in April, he sings his song in May;
In the middle of June he changes his tune,
In July he flies away.*

Tulips and narcissi bloom in a garland for an April birthday card. Other flowers of the month selected for band and border motifs include violets and forget-me-nots, and my favourite lily of the valley.

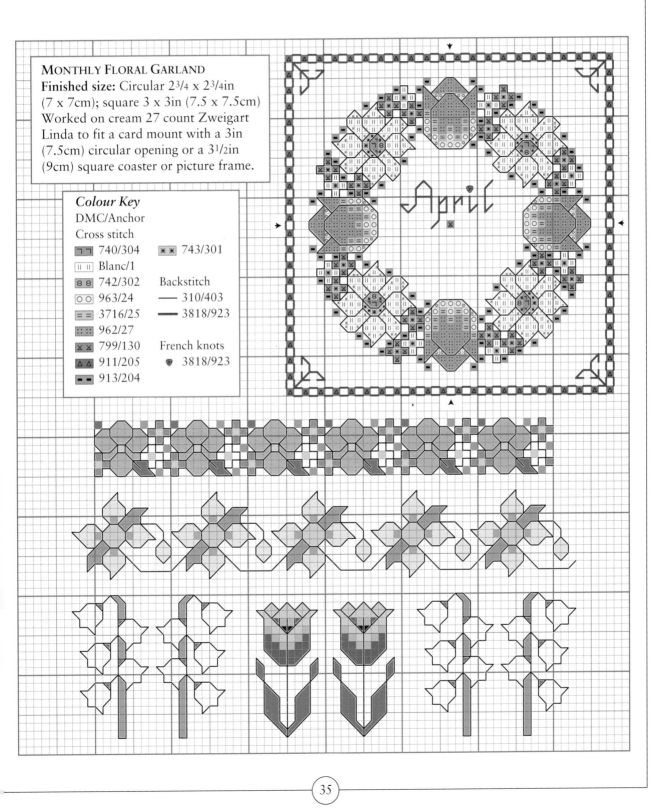

MONTHLY FLORAL GARLAND
Finished size: Circular 2¾ x 2¾in (7 x 7cm); square 3 x 3in (7.5 x 7.5cm) Worked on cream 27 count Zweigart Linda to fit a card mount with a 3in (7.5cm) circular opening or a 3½in (9cm) square coaster or picture frame.

Colour Key
DMC/Anchor
Cross stitch
740/304
Blanc/1
88 742/302
963/24
3716/25
962/27
799/130
911/205
913/204
743/301

Backstitch
— 310/403
— 3818/923

French knots
3818/923

Don't let St George's Day go unnoticed. Stitch the patron saint of England with a ferocious dragon, or if you are of a nervous disposition you may prefer to stitch the gentle English roses.

Aries (21st March – 20th April)

Feast Day – Easter

23rd April: St George's Day

The Paschal candle and lilies celebrate Easter, which often falls in April. The Easter bunnies, below, are a reminder that carrots are better for me than Easter eggs.

A day out at the races is enjoyed by many when the world famous Grand National steeplechase is run at Aintree.

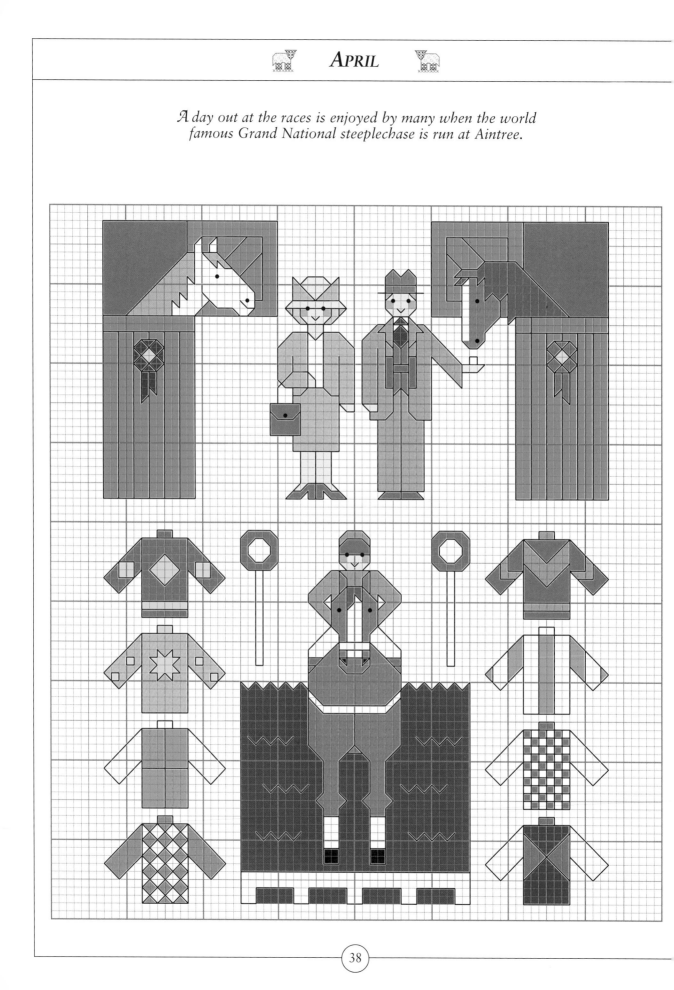

*Stitch a spring-cleaning sampler with a yellow duster border and
you will have the perfect excuse to ignore the housework.*

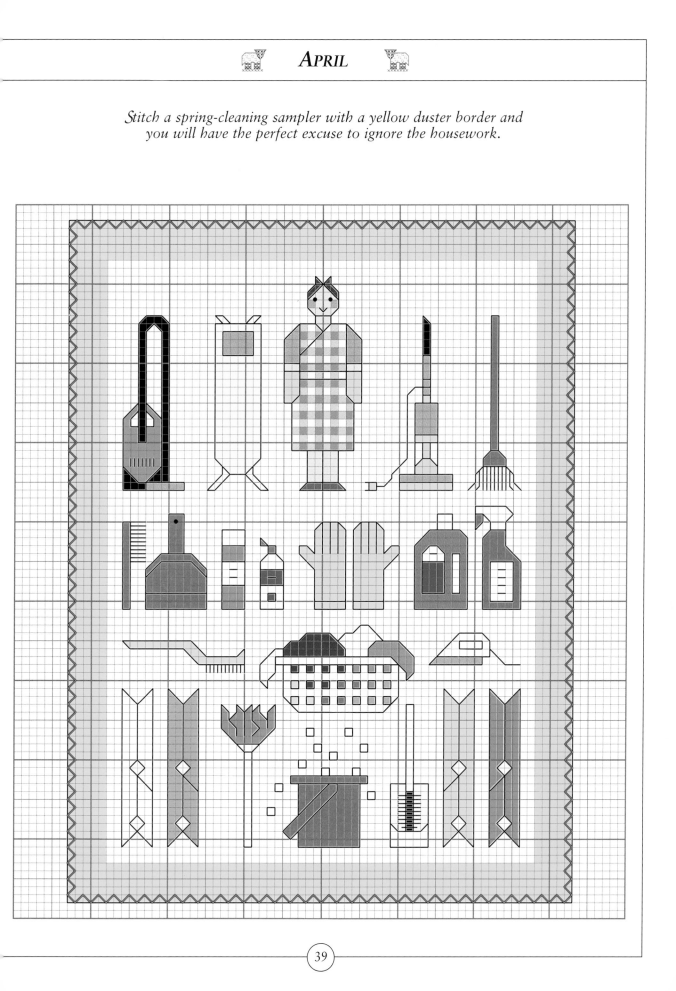

MAY

He that would live forever must eat sage in May.

Daisies and bluebells, primroses and violets for a May birthday card, with other seasonal flowers for bands and borders to brighten your stitching.

MONTHLY FLORAL GARLAND
Finished size: Circular 2³/4 x 2³/4in
(7 x 7cm); square 3 x 3in (7.5 x 7.5cm)
Worked on cream 27 count Zweigart
Linda to fit a card mount with a 3in
(7.5cm) circular opening or a 3¹/2in
(9cm) square coaster or picture frame.

Colour Key
DMC/Anchor

Cross stitch		Backstitch	
⌐⌐	340/118	—	310/403
II II	Blanc/1	—	3818/923
\ \	799/130	—	961/76
△ △	911/205		
▪ ▪	563/208		French knots
⊠ ⊠	745/293	⊛	743/297
✳ ✳	743/297		

Gardeners rejoice at the coming of May and the chance to visit London's inspirational Chelsea Flower Show once again. The long-awaited asparagus is now in season too.

Taurus (21st April – 21st May)

A B C D E F G H I J K L M N
O P Q R S T U V W X Y Z
1st 2nd 3rd 4th 5 6 7 8 9 0

Feast Day – Pentecost (Whit Sunday)

Traditionally May Day is a time to celebrate the end of winter and the arrival of spring. On village greens throughout the land children dance weaving their ribbons around the maypole.

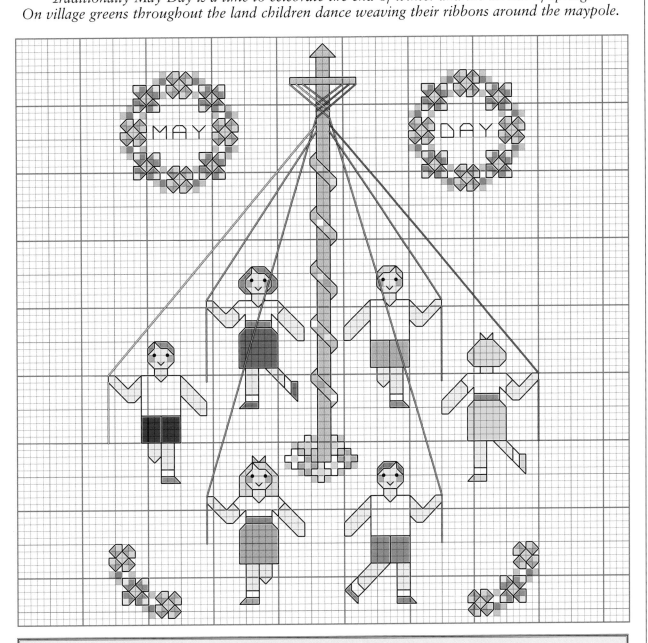

MAY DAY PICTURE
(photographed on page 40)

Finished size: 5 x 6¼in (13 x 16cm). Worked on white 27 count Linda. For the ribbons, use Offray 2mm embroidery ribbon in the colours of your choice and apply them to the embroidery in the positions shown on the chart.

If you work them in order, one right then one left then one right and so on in sequence, they will weave realistically around the pole. Alternatively you could use long lengths of six-strand stranded cotton in the same way.

The F. A. Cup Final takes place in May. Change the team colours and you can immortalise your local soccer team in cross stitch, even if they do not make it to Wembley.

Time to play...stitch this clock for a sporting fan and they will never be late for the game.

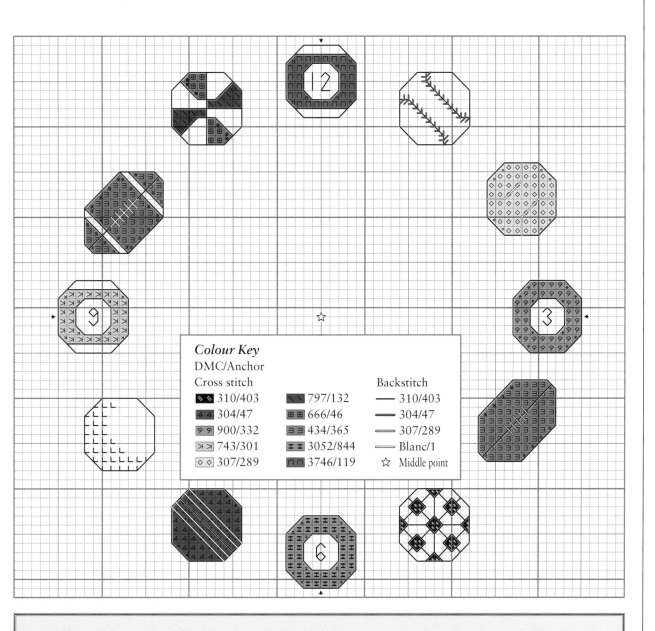

Colour Key

DMC/Anchor

Cross stitch				Backstitch	
◣◥	310/403	◣◥	797/132	——	310/403
4 4	304/47	⊞⊞	666/46	——	304/47
9 9	900/332	⌿⌿	434/365	——	307/289
⋗⋗	743/301	⊥⊥	3052/844	——	Blanc/1
◇◇	307/289	⊓⊓	3746/119	☆	Middle point

SPORTING CLOCK
(photographed on page 40)

Finished size: 4¹/₄ x 4¹/₄in (11 x 11cm).
Worked on 28 count white Jobelan to fit a wooden frame with a 5 x 5in (13 x 13cm) aperture. The frame was covered with self-adhesive green baize to simulate a field of play and white ribbon was added to represent pitch markings. Quartz battery-operated clock movements are available from hobby shops. When the work had been mounted, a hole was made at the point marked ☆ on the chart and the clock movement was inserted.

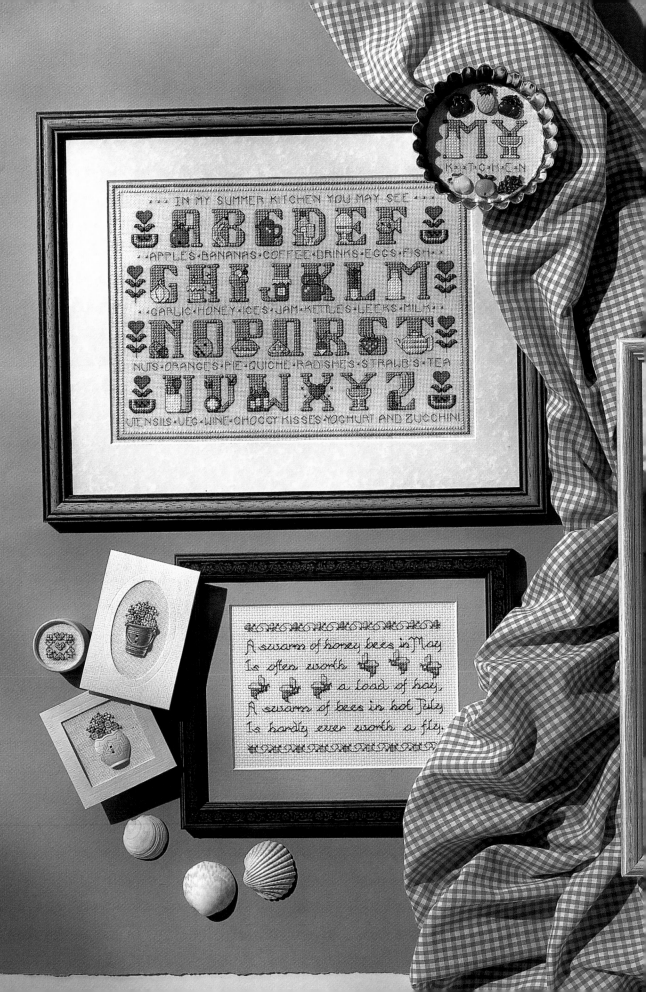

SUMMER

An English summer, three hot days then a thunderstorm.

Stitch-off-the-page designs to celebrate the season of summer.

SUMMER ALPHABET
(charted on pages 48–49)
Finished size: 9³/4 x 7¹/4in (25 x 18.5cm).
Worked on cream 27 count Zweigart Linda. Letters from the alphabet can be extracted to stitch initials, names or events through the season.

SUMMER BAND SAMPLER
(charted on page 50)
Finished size: 3¹/2 x 9¹/2in (9 x 24cm).
Worked on 28 count Country Style Evenweave (NJ449.20).
When work is complete, stitch a seasonal brass charm onto the heart at the bottom of the design. To prevent tarnishing, clean brass charms with alcohol and seal them with a thin coat of clear varnish before applying them to embroidery. Frame the sampler or hang it from bell-pull ends to make a small hanging.

SUMMER WEATHER FOLKLORE
(charted on page 51)
Finished size: 5¹/2 x 3³/4in (14 x 9.5cm).
Worked on cream 14 count Zweigart Aida.

THE GARDEN IN SUMMER
(charted on page 52, photographed on page 53)
Finished size: 6 x 6³/4in (15 x 17cm).
Worked on 28 count Country Style Evenweave (NJ449.20).

Summer Alphabet, Summer Band Sampler and Summer Weather Folklore, plus other items from this season. Each month also has a photograph showing a variety of completed pieces to give you some ideas on how the charts may be used

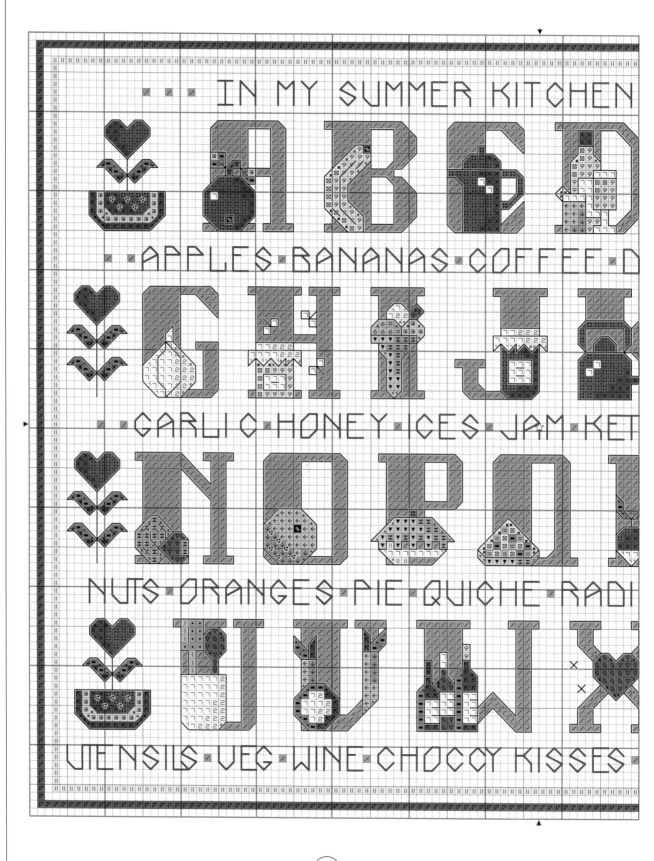

IN MY SUMMER KITCHEN

APPLES · BANANAS · COFFEE · D

GARLIC · HONEY · ICES · JAM · KET

NUTS · ORANGES · PIE · QUICHE · RADI

UTENSILS · VEG · WINE · CHOCCY KISSES

Summer Alphabet

Colour Key

DMC/Anchor
Cross stitch

·· ·	414/235
◣◥	310/403
⊓⊓	Blanc/1
ǀ ǀ	415/398
ǁ ǁ	800/128
2 2	746/386
6 6	604/60
9 9	726/295
⠿	304/47
= =	603/62
◤◤	798/131
⁄ ⁄	799/130
✕✕	815/1005
↓↓	740/304
←←	741/303
▽▽	801/359
◨◨	433/371
▬▬	911/205
▣▣	955/1043
◤◤	909/245
⊠⊠	727/292
⊞⊞	436/363
▼▼	437/361

Backstitch

— 310/403
— 797/132

French knots

🌀 310/403
🌀 726/295

☆ Middle point

*A full moon
brings fair
weather.*

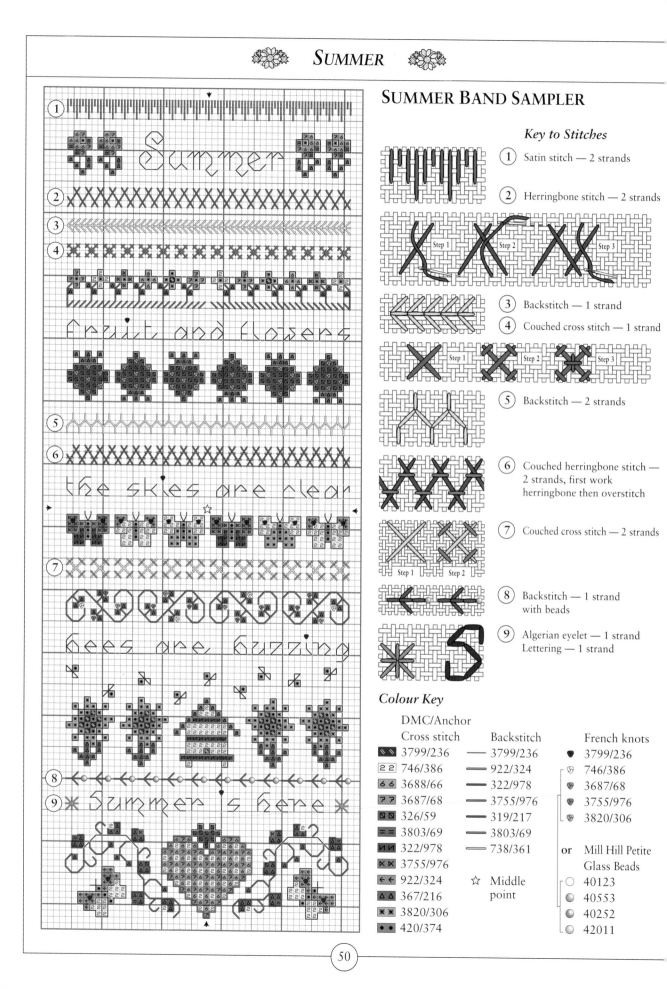

SUMMER BAND SAMPLER

Key to Stitches

1. Satin stitch — 2 strands
2. Herringbone stitch — 2 strands
3. Backstitch — 1 strand
4. Couched cross stitch — 1 strand
5. Backstitch — 2 strands
6. Couched herringbone stitch — 2 strands, first work herringbone then overstitch
7. Couched cross stitch — 2 strands
8. Backstitch — 1 strand with beads
9. Algerian eyelet — 1 strand Lettering — 1 strand

Colour Key

DMC/Anchor

Cross stitch	Backstitch	French knots
3799/236	— 3799/236	♥ 3799/236
746/386	— 922/324	♥ 746/386
3688/66	— 322/978	♥ 3687/68
3687/68	— 3755/976	♥ 3755/976
326/59	— 319/217	♥ 3820/306
3803/69	— 3803/69	
322/978	— 738/361	or Mill Hill Petite
3755/976		Glass Beads
922/324	☆ Middle	○ 40123
367/216	point	● 40553
3820/306		● 40252
420/374		● 42011

> *A swarm of honey bees in May*
> *Is often worth a load of hay,*
> *A swarm of bees in hot July*
> *Is hardly ever worth a fly.*

SUMMER WEATHER FOLKLORE

Colour Key

DMC/Anchor

Cross stitch				Backstitch	French knots
Blanc/1	745/386	725/306		— 310/403	310/403
703/238	721/324	783/307		— 700/239	Blanc/1
700/239	780/310			☆ Middle point	

Fine weather in June sets corn in tune.

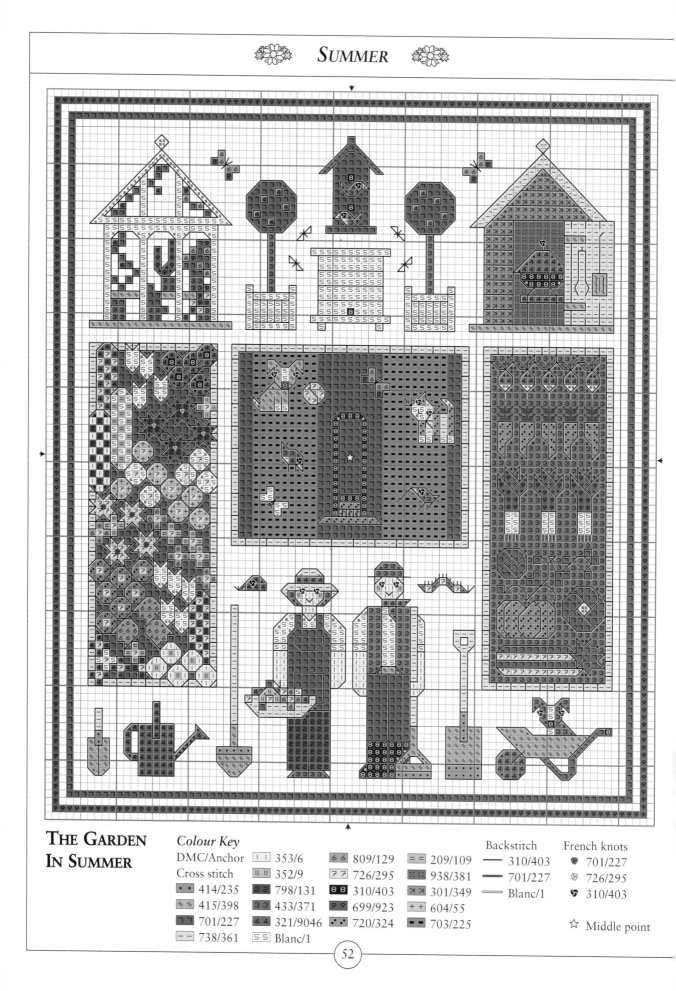

THE GARDEN IN SUMMER

Colour Key

DMC/Anchor

Cross stitch

⊥⊥	353/6	⬡⬡	809/129	= =	209/109	
⊪⊪	352/9	◪◪	726/295	◌◌◌	938/381	
••••	414/235	22	798/131	88	310/403	➤➤ 301/349
◩◩	415/398	33	433/371	⬢⬢	699/923	++ 604/55
◪1	701/227	44	321/9046	•◌•	720/324	▬▬ 703/225
− −	738/361	55	Blanc/1			

Backstitch
— 310/403
— 701/227
═ Blanc/1

French knots
❦ 701/227
❧ 726/295
🌀 310/403

☆ Middle point

JUNE

Look at your corn in May, and you'll come weeping away;
Look at your corn in June and you'll come home to another tune.

Delicate dog roses appear in the hedgerows and feature in the design for this month's birthday card. Beneath are more band and border designs suitable for early summer.

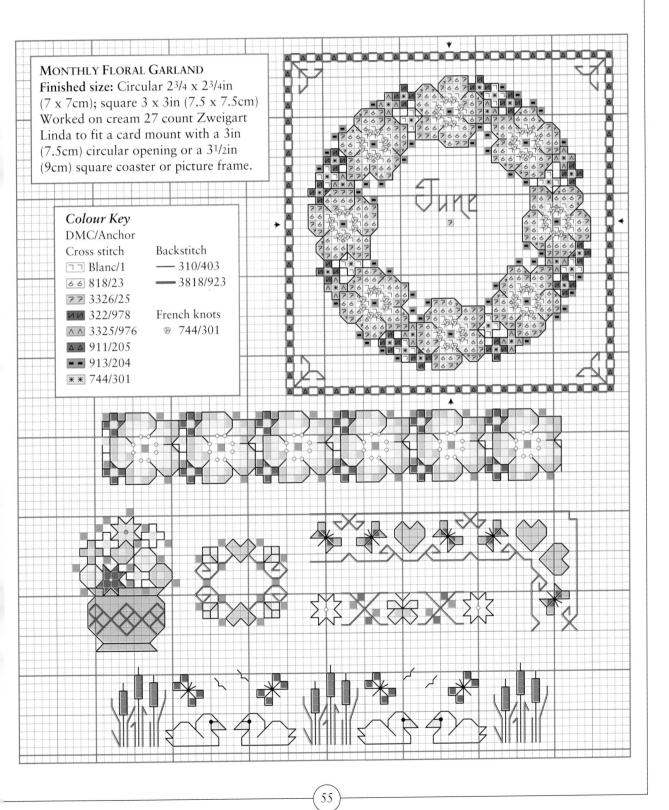

MONTHLY FLORAL GARLAND

Finished size: Circular 2³/₄ x 2³/₄in (7 x 7cm); square 3 x 3in (7.5 x 7.5cm) Worked on cream 27 count Zweigart Linda to fit a card mount with a 3in (7.5cm) circular opening or a 3¹/₂in (9cm) square coaster or picture frame.

Colour Key

DMC/Anchor

Cross stitch		Backstitch	
⊓⊓	Blanc/1	——	310/403
6 6	818/23	━━	3818/923
7 7	3326/25		
и и	322/978	French knots	
∧ ∧	3325/976	✿	744/301
△ △	911/205		
- -	913/204		
✳ ✳	744/301		

*A zodiac sign, June roses and other designs to celebrate
high days and holy days that fall this month.*

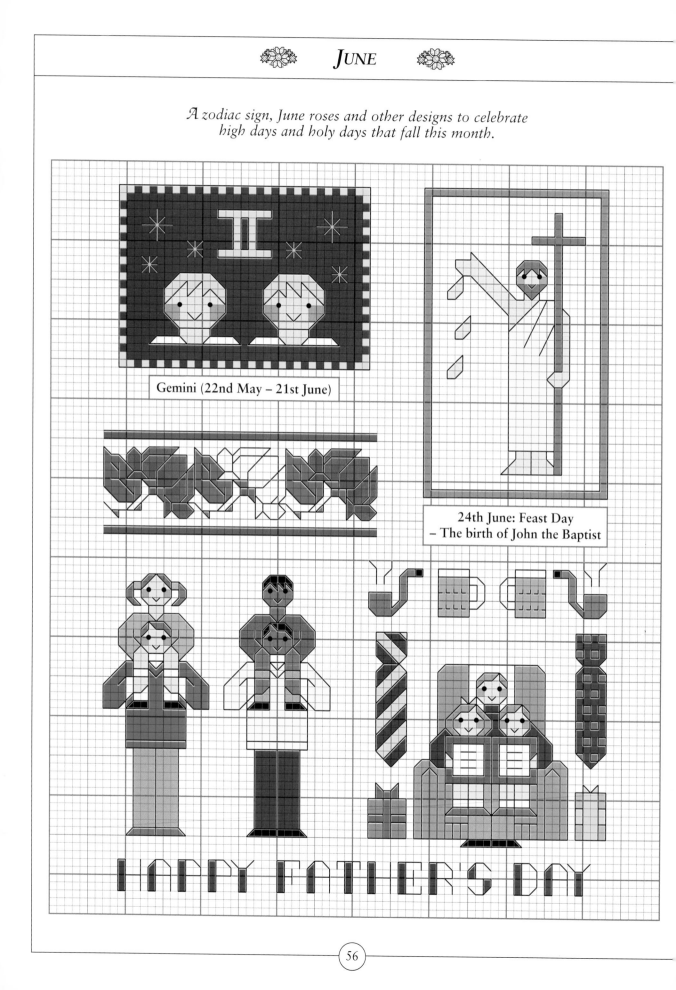

Gemini (22nd May – 21st June)

24th June: Feast Day
– The birth of John the Baptist

*In June the coarse fishing season opens. Even if the
fish are elusive, the riverbanks teem with wildlife.*

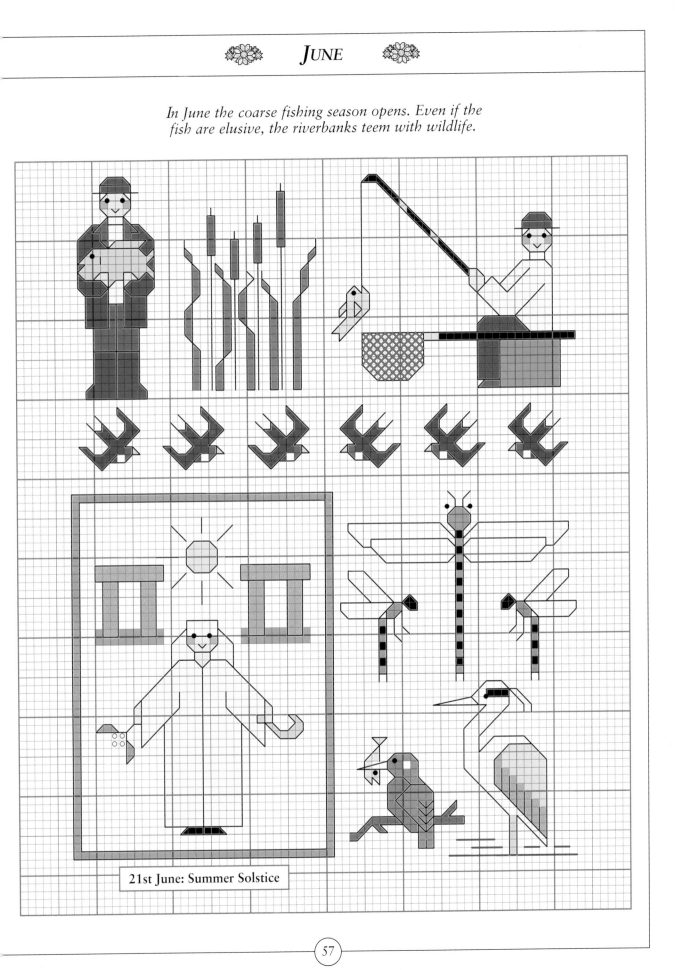

21st June: Summer Solstice

Time for tennis enthusiasts to enjoy a bowl of strawberries and lobs and volleys at the Wimbledon Lawn Tennis Championships, while motor sport fanatics attend the Le Mans 24-hour sports car endurance race.

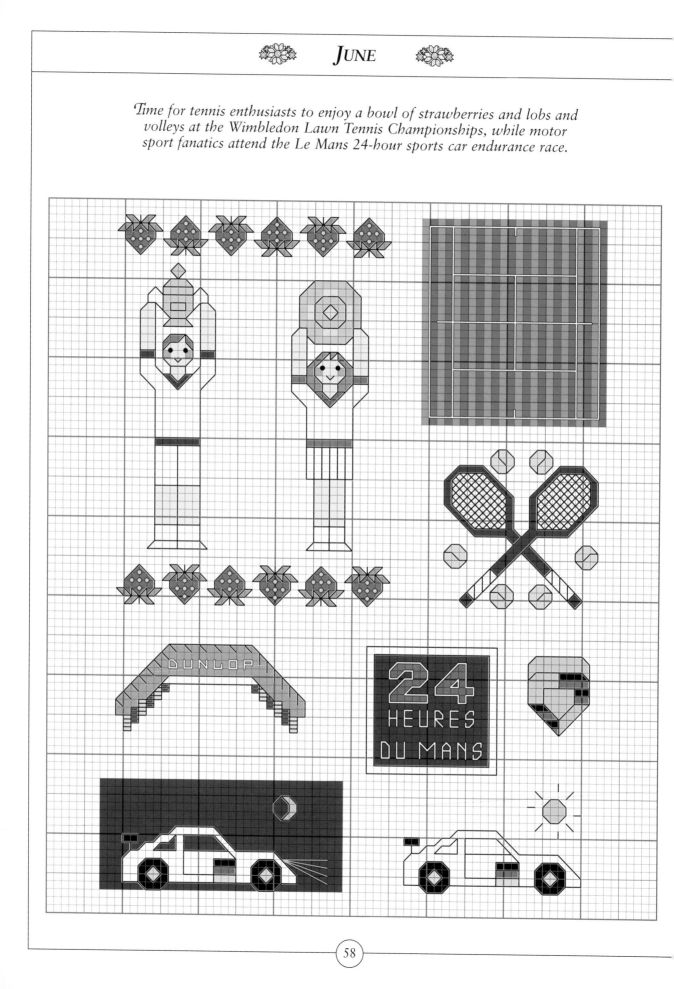

June is the most popular month for weddings. Whilst the groom's mother wipes away a tear the other participants smile for the camera.

JULY

*If the first of July it be rainy weather,
'Twill rain, more or less for four weeks together.*

A ring of summer flowers for the July birthday card and beneath it several border designs full of butterflies and flowers to frame your chosen July motifs.

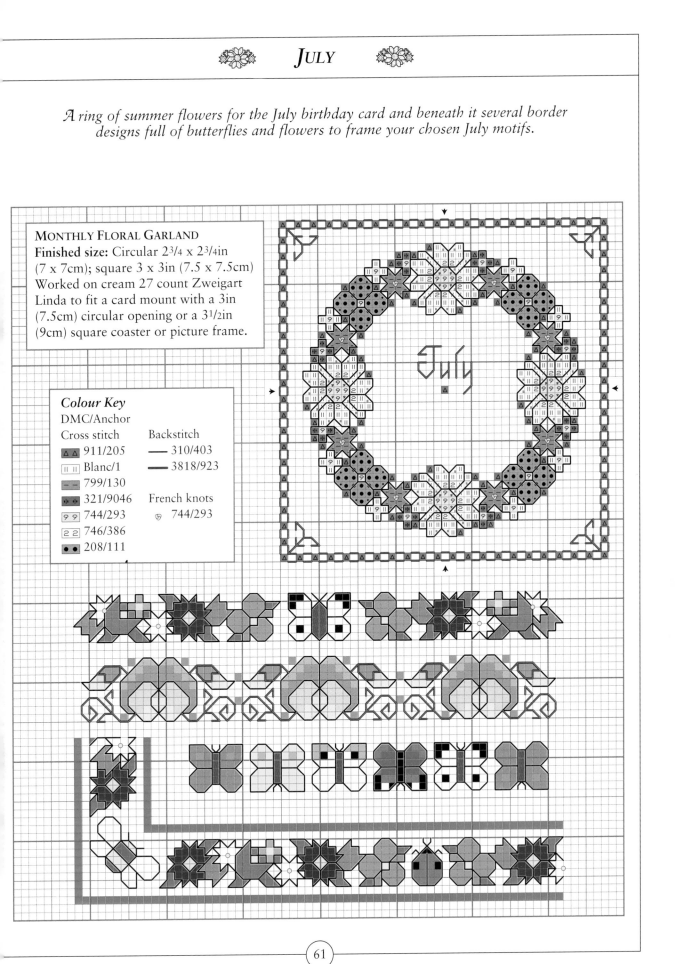

MONTHLY FLORAL GARLAND

Finished size: Circular 2³/4 x 2³/4in (7 x 7cm); square 3 x 3in (7.5 x 7.5cm) Worked on cream 27 count Zweigart Linda to fit a card mount with a 3in (7.5cm) circular opening or a 3¹/2in (9cm) square coaster or picture frame.

Colour Key

DMC/Anchor

Cross stitch		Backstitch	
△ △	911/205	——	310/403
‖ ‖	Blanc/1	——	3818/923
– –	799/130		
•‖• •‖•	321/9046	French knots	
9 9	744/293	ꝯ	744/293
2 2	746/386		
•• ••	208/111		

*Charted below are motifs for just a few of the important
dates to remember in the month of July.*

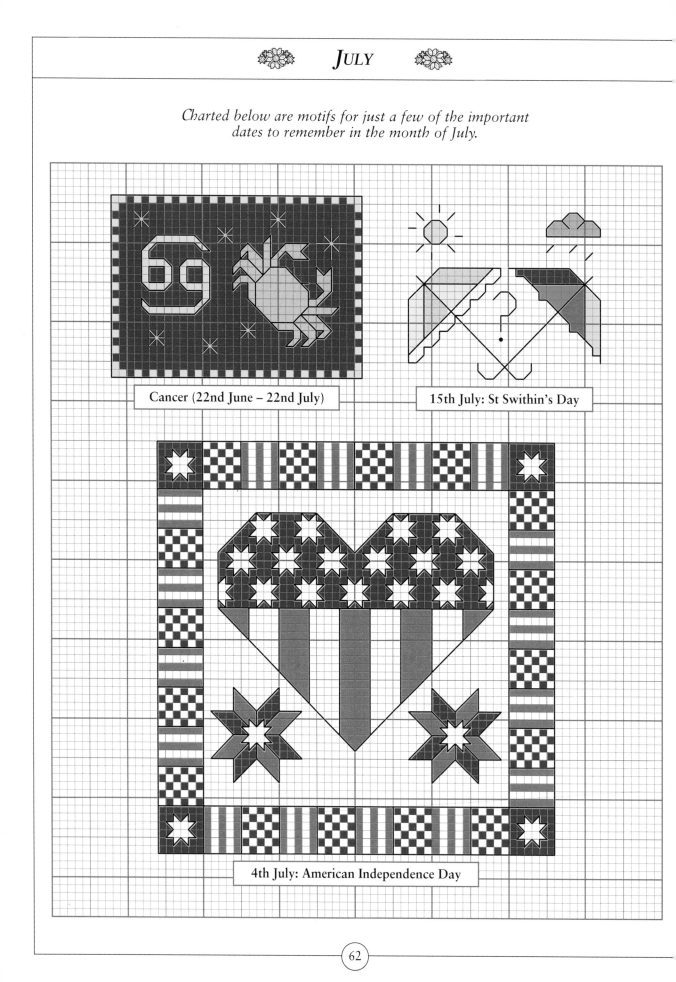

Cancer (22nd June – 22nd July)

15th July: St Swithin's Day

4th July: American Independence Day

Summer days are not complete without the humming of bees,
and picnics are not picnics without ants.

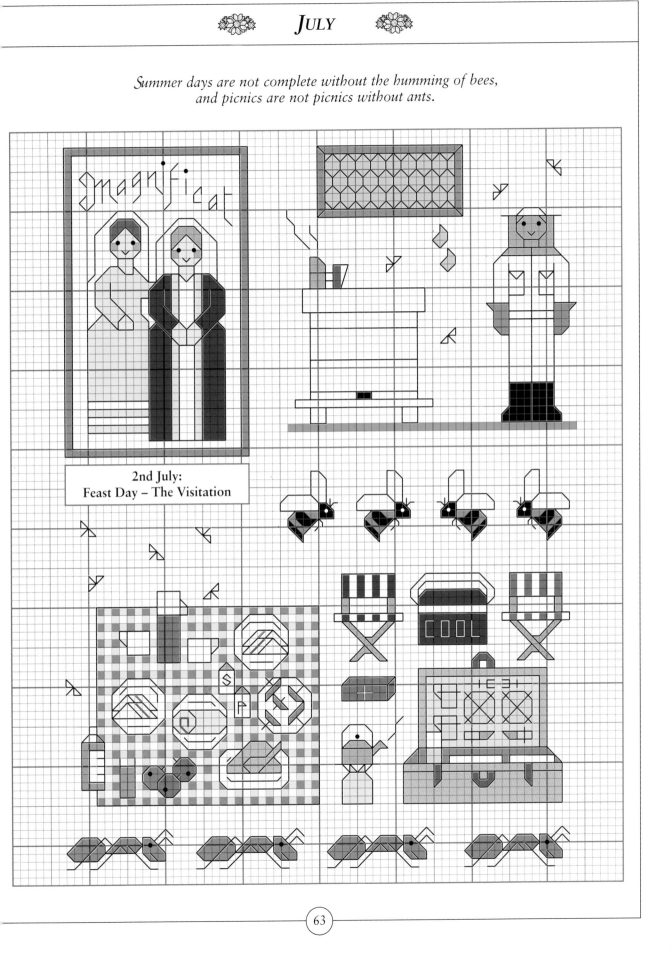

2nd July:
Feast Day – The Visitation

An important motoring event, the British Grand Prix
is held at Silverstone in July. To depict any other
Grand Prix simply change the national flag.

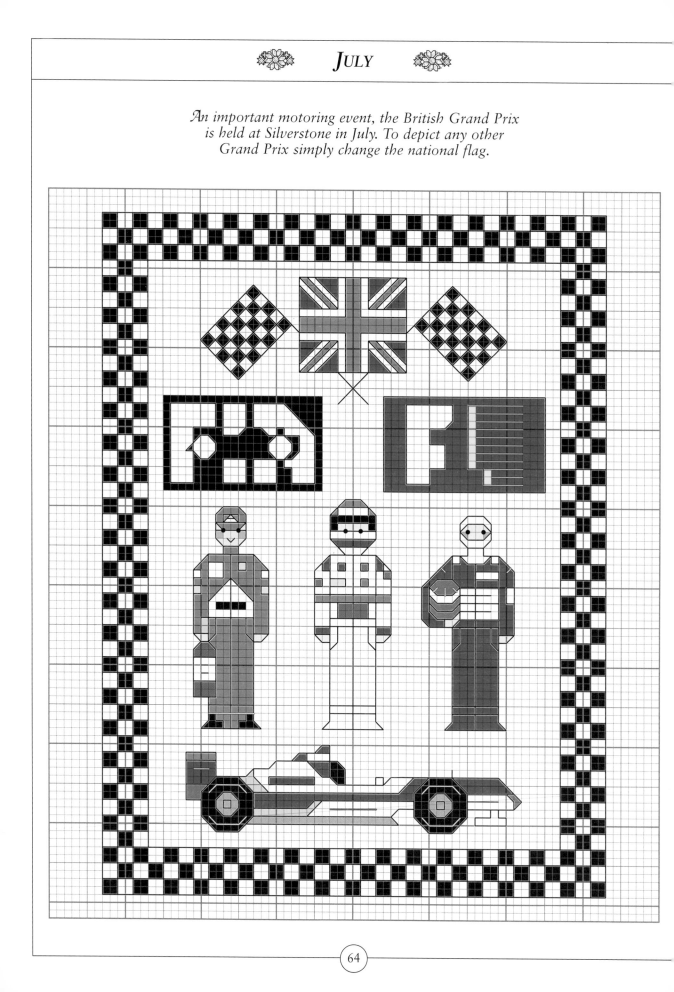

The warm summer weather brings out the sportsperson in everyone,
whether they are a champion at the school sports day or competing
in the world's most famous cycling race, the Tour de France.

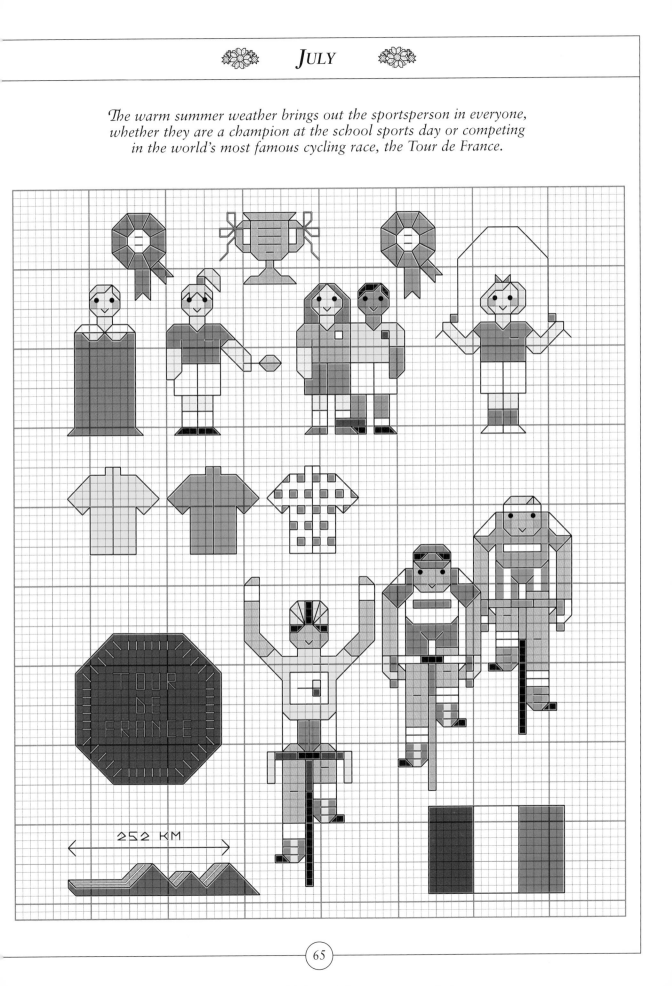

AUGUST

❀ ❀

*If the twenty fourth of August be fair and clear,
Then hope for a prosperous autumn that year.*

Poppies, cornflowers and pimpernels have been borrowed from the cornfields to create the August birthday card garland. Fuschias and sunflowers are a common sight in our gardens this month.

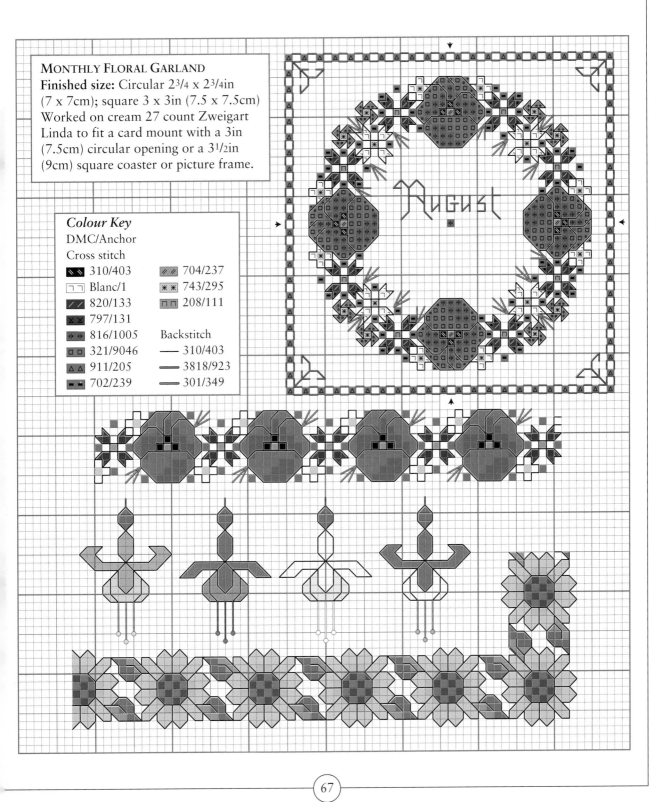

MONTHLY FLORAL GARLAND
Finished size: Circular 2³/4 x 2³/4in
(7 x 7cm); square 3 x 3in (7.5 x 7.5cm)
Worked on cream 27 count Zweigart
Linda to fit a card mount with a 3in
(7.5cm) circular opening or a 3¹/2in
(9cm) square coaster or picture frame.

Colour Key
DMC/Anchor
Cross stitch
310/403
Blanc/1
820/133
797/131
816/1005
321/9046
911/205
702/239
704/237
743/295
208/111

Backstitch
—— 310/403
—— 3818/923
—— 301/349

Families rediscover the great outdoors, while musicians and dancers from all over the world congregate at the Welsh town of Llangollen for the annual International Music Eisteddfod.

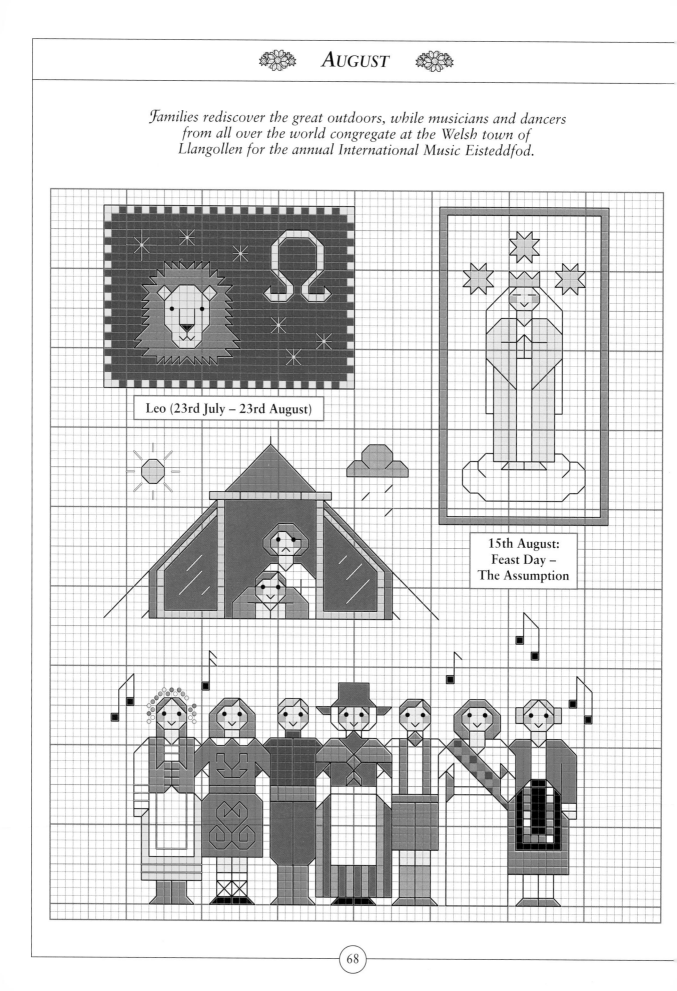

Leo (23rd July – 23rd August)

15th August:
Feast Day –
The Assumption

Traditional summer entertainments: Punch & Judy booths spring up on the beaches to entertain the children, and Morris dancers appear on village greens everywhere baffling foreign visitors.

The peaceful cricket match, whether at Lords or in the local village, is a relaxing way to spend a summer's day, with a break for afternoon tea.

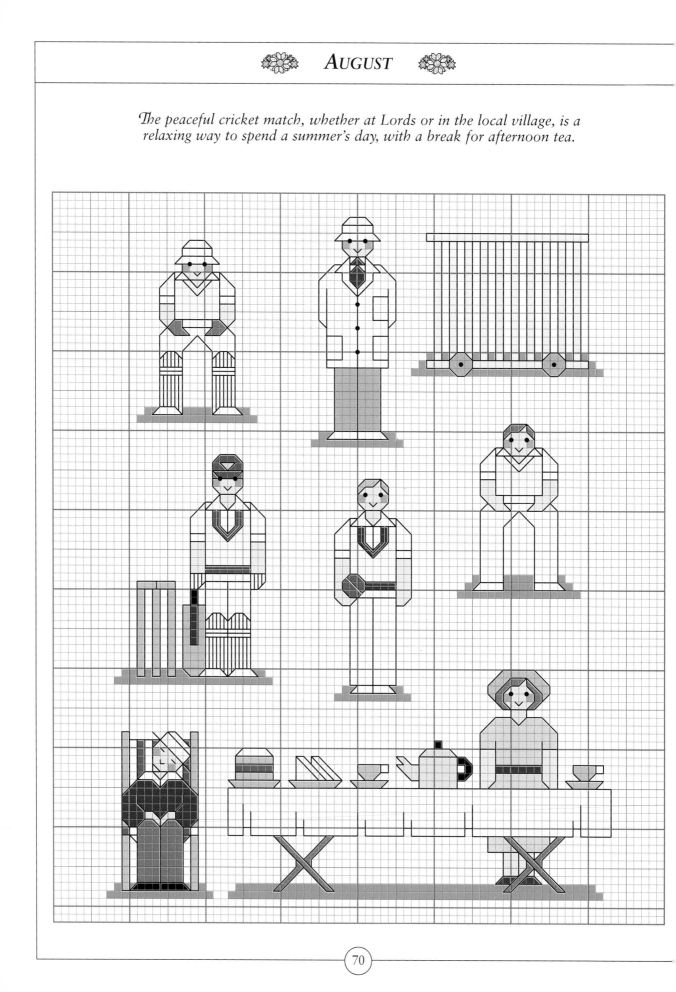

Sunny days are spent at the beach, building sandcastles, collecting shells and eating cooling ice cream. Shades and sun cream are a must.

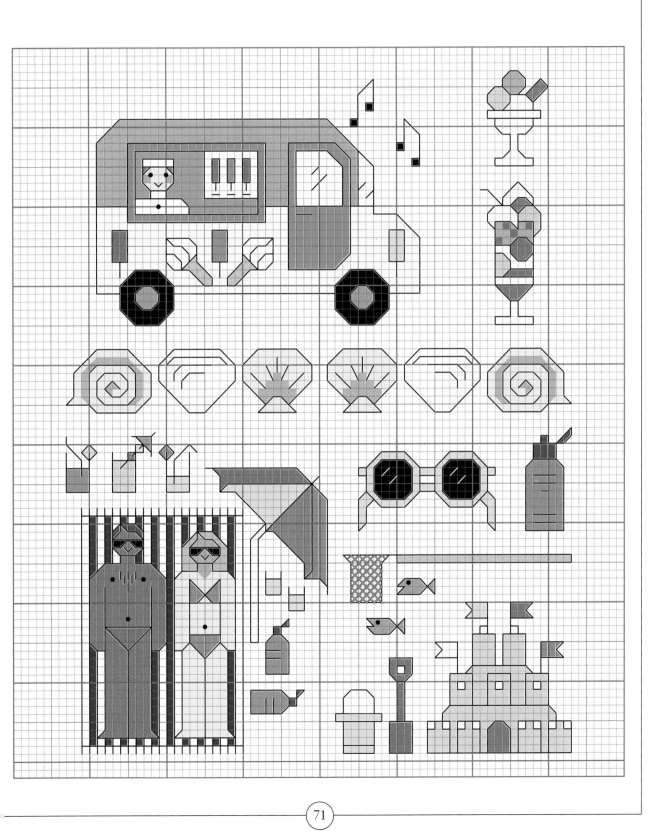

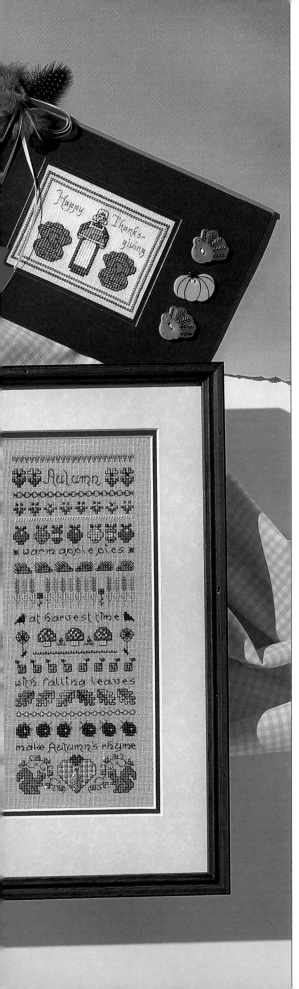

❧ AUTUMN ❧

*Evening red and morning grey
Help the traveller on his way;
Evening grey and morning red
Bring down rain upon his head.*

*Stitch-off-the-page designs to
celebrate the season of autumn*

AUTUMN ALPHABET
(charted on pages 74–75)
Finished size: 9³/4 x 7¹/4in (25 x 18.5cm).
Worked on cream 27 count Zweigart Linda.
Letters from the alphabet can be extracted
to stitch initials, names or events through
the season.

AUTUMN BAND SAMPLER
(charted on page 76)
Finished size: 3¹/2 x 9¹/2in (9 x 24cm).
Worked on 28 count Country Style
Evenweave (NJ449.16).
When work is complete, stitch a seasonal
brass charm onto the heart at the bottom of
the design. To prevent tarnishing, clean brass
charms with alcohol and seal them with a thin
coat of clear varnish before applying them to
embroidery. Frame the sampler or hang it
from bell-pull ends to make a small hanging.

AUTUMN WEATHER FOLKLORE
(charted on page 77)
Finished size: 5¹/2 x 3³/4in (14 x 9.5cm).
Worked on 14 count Zweigart Rustico Aida.

THE GARDEN IN AUTUMN
(charted on page 78, photographed on page 79)
Finished size: 6 x 6³/4in (15 x 17cm).
Worked on 28 count Country Style
Evenweave (NJ449.20).

*Autumn Alphabet, Autumn Band Sampler and Autumn
Weather Folklore, plus other items from this season. Each
month also has a photograph showing a variety of completed
pieces to give you some ideas on how the charts may be used*

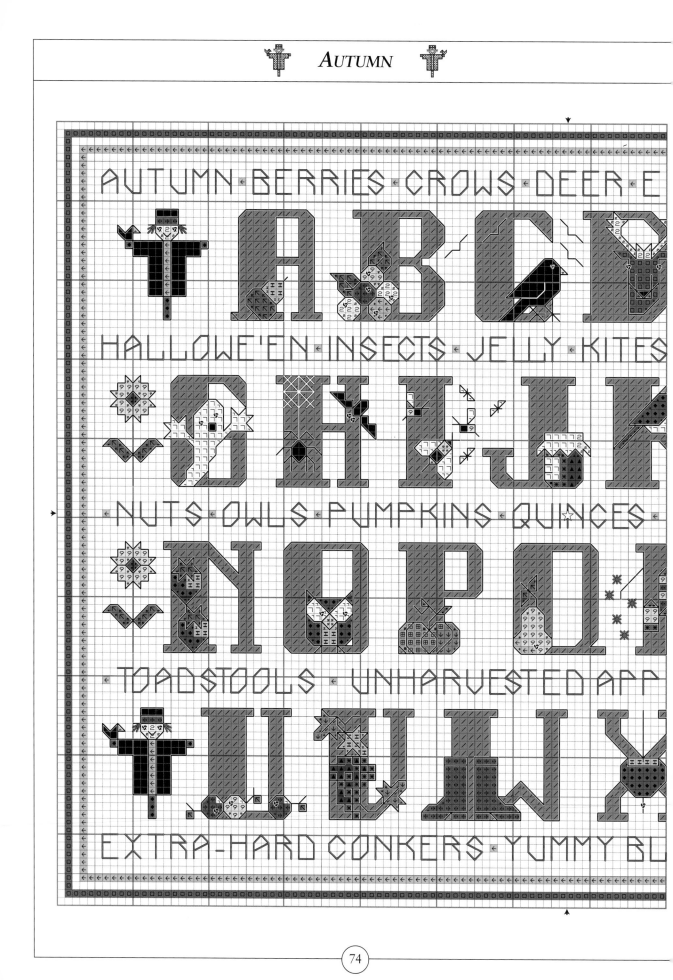

AUTUMN ← BERRIES · CROWS · DEER · E

A B C D

HALLOWE'EN ← INSECTS ← JELLY · KITES

G H I J K

· NUTS ← OWLS ← PUMPKINS ← QUINCES ·

N O P Q

· TOADSTOOLS · UNHARVESTED APP

T U V W X

EXTRA-HARD CONKERS · YUMMY BL

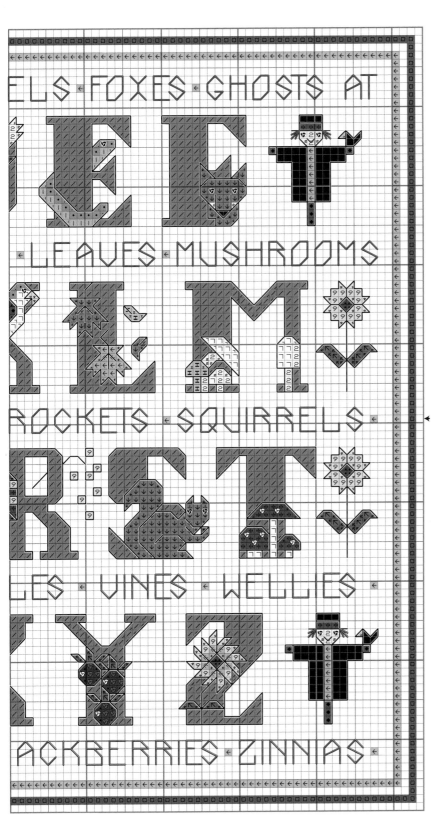

AUTUMN ALPHABET

Colour Key

DMC/Anchor
Cross stitch

• •	414/235
■	310/403
⊤ ⊤	Blanc/1
I I	415/398
2 2	746/386
9 9	3822/305
⁄⁄	470/266
⪡ ⪡	347/13
□ ⊡	920/339
⊞ ⊞	721/324
↓ ↓	720/326
← ←	3820/306
◹ ◹	367/216
✳ ✳	327/100
◆ ◆	898/360
I I	437/368
▲ ▲	550/102

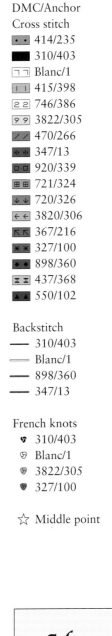

Backstitch

— 310/403
═ Blanc/1
— 898/360
— 347/13

French knots

🌀 310/403
🌀 Blanc/1
🌀 3822/305
🌀 327/100

☆ Middle point

Mackerel sky,
Not long dry.

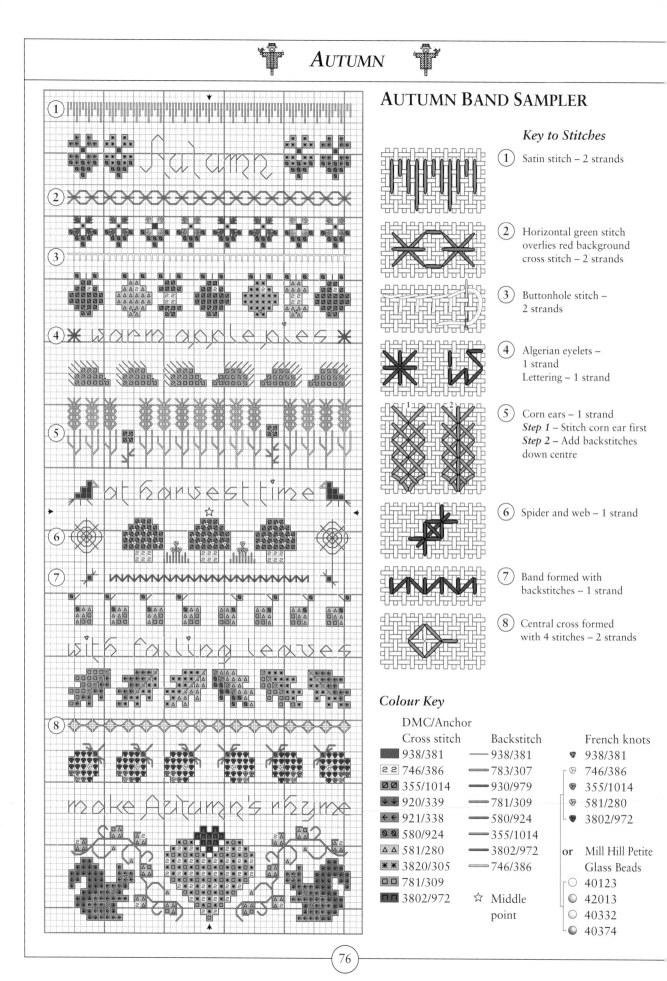

AUTUMN BAND SAMPLER

Key to Stitches

1. Satin stitch – 2 strands

2. Horizontal green stitch overlies red background cross stitch – 2 strands

3. Buttonhole stitch – 2 strands

4. Algerian eyelets – 1 strand
   Lettering – 1 strand

5. Corn ears – 1 strand
   Step 1 – Stitch corn ear first
   Step 2 – Add backstitches down centre

6. Spider and web – 1 strand

7. Band formed with backstitches – 1 strand

8. Central cross formed with 4 stitches – 2 strands

Colour Key

DMC/Anchor

Cross stitch	Backstitch	French knots
938/381	—938/381	938/381
2 2 746/386	—783/307	746/386
☑ ☑ 355/1014	—930/979	355/1014
↓↓ 920/339	—781/309	581/280
←← 921/338	—580/924	3802/972
☒ ☒ 580/924	—355/1014	
△△ 581/280	—3802/972	**or** Mill Hill Petite
✳ ✳ 3820/305	—746/386	Glass Beads
☐ ☐ 781/309		40123
☐ ☐ 3802/972	☆ Middle point	42013
		40332
		40374

> *When the wind is in the north*
> *The skillful fisher goes not forth*
> *When the wind is in the south*
> *It blows the bait in the fish's mouth.*

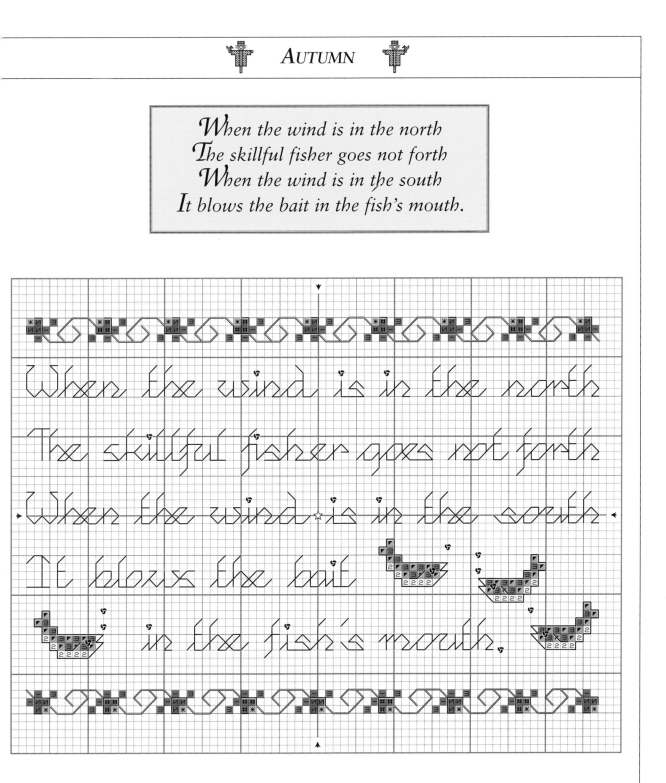

AUTUMN WEATHER FOLKLORE

Colour Key
DMC/Anchor

Cross stitch

367/216	434/365	327/100
746/386	436/363	
347/13	3820/307	

Backstitch
— 310/403
— 367/216
☆ Middle point

French knots
🌀 310/403

> *In the old of the moon*
> *A cloudy morning*
> *Bodes a fair afternoon.*

THE GARDEN IN AUTUMN

Colour Key

DMC/Anchor

Cross stitch

`· ·`	414/235	`4 4`	321/9046	`0 0`	720/324		
`\ \`	415/398	`5 5`	Blanc/1	`= =`	301/349		
`7 7`	701/227	`7 7`	726/295	`:::`	938/381		
`- -`	738/361	`8 8`	310/403	`> >`	746/386		
`l l`	353/6	`9 9`	699/923	`◇ ◇`	915/1029		
`ll ll`	352/9						
`1 1`	701/227	`3 3`	433/371				

Backstitch
— 310/403
— 300/357
— 798/131
— 701/227
— 209/109
— 746/386

French knots
☙ Blanc/1
☙ 726/295
❣ 310/403
☙ 746/386

☆ Middle point

SEPTEMBER

*September blows soft
Till the fruit's in the loft.*

Rudbeckias, gazanias and Michaelmas daisies herald the coming of autumn in September's birthday card garland. Apples are picked and eaten or polished up as presents for teachers on the return to school.

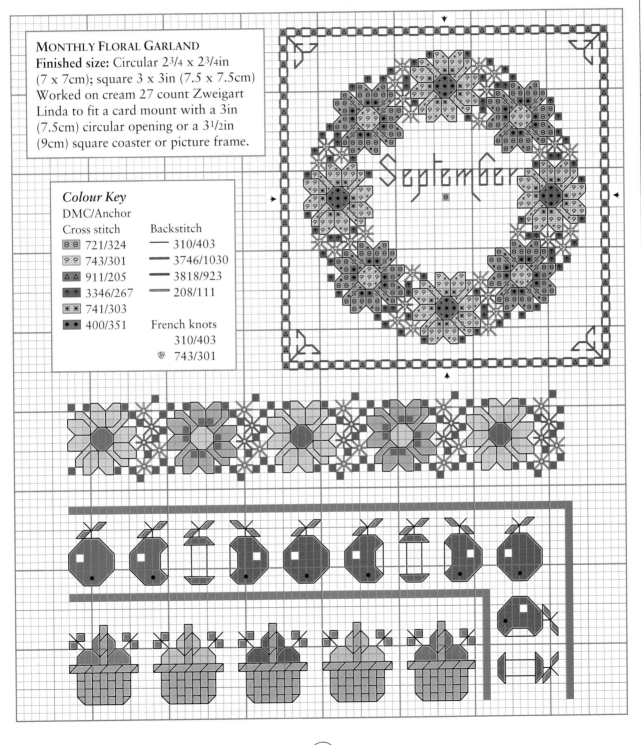

MONTHLY FLORAL GARLAND
Finished size: Circular 2³/₄ x 2³/₄in (7 x 7cm); square 3 x 3in (7.5 x 7.5cm) Worked on cream 27 count Zweigart Linda to fit a card mount with a 3in (7.5cm) circular opening or a 3¹/₂in (9cm) square coaster or picture frame.

Colour Key
DMC/Anchor

Cross stitch	Backstitch
88 721/324	— 310/403
99 743/301	═ 3746/1030
△△ 911/205	═ 3818/923
↑↑ 3346/267	═ 208/111
✳✳ 741/303	
◆◆ 400/351	French knots
	310/403
	◈ 743/301

In September the Henry Wood Promenade Concerts take place at the Albert Hall in London, and the last night of the Proms gives music lovers the chance to let their hair down.

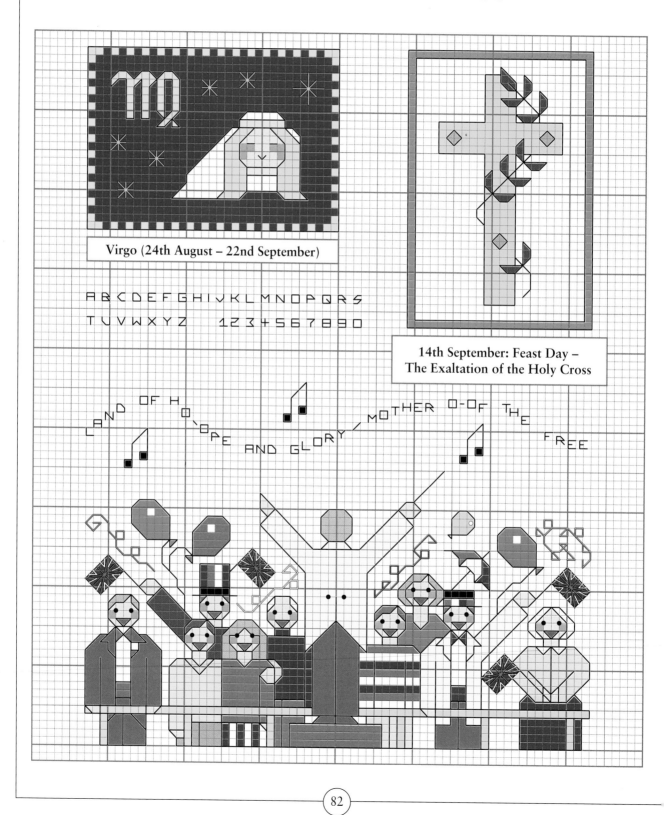

Virgo (24th August – 22nd September)

ABCDEFGHIJKLMNOPQRS
TUVWXYZ   1234567890

**14th September: Feast Day –
The Exaltation of the Holy Cross**

LAND OF HO-OPE AND GLORY MOTHER O-OF THE FREE

After a fruitful summer the jam-making season has arrived. In village halls across the country local horticultural societies hold their annual shows and rosettes are awarded to the finest produce. Meanwhile, in Scotland the Highland Games are in full swing.

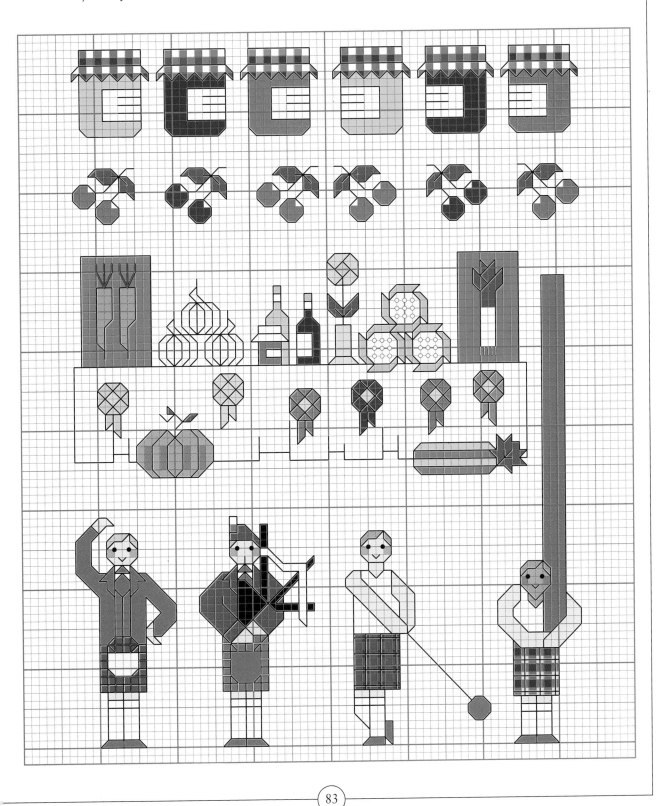

Out on the golf course the players strive to emulate the professionals who are competing for the Ryder Cup during this month.

*September sees children returning to school for the new academic year.
New teachers are introduced, new games are played in the playground,
and lessons are learnt more willingly by some than by others.*

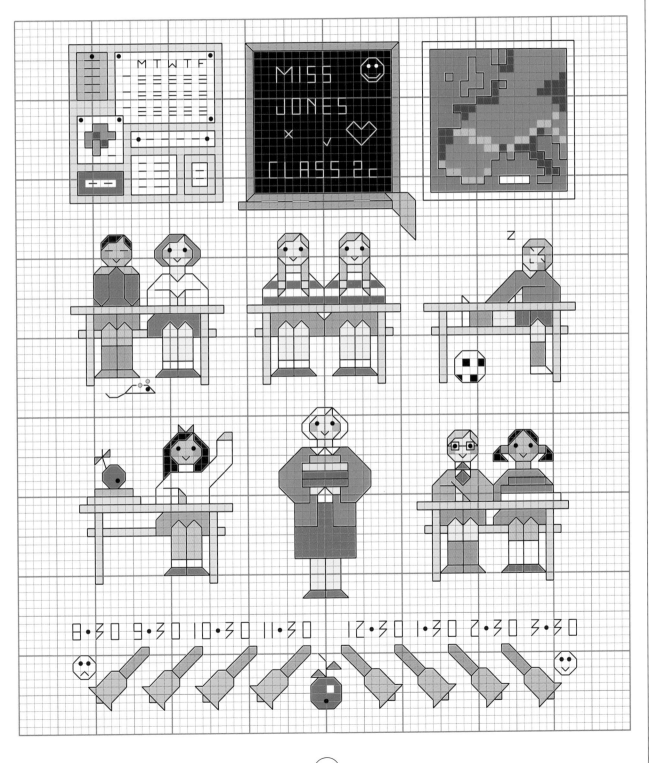

OCTOBER

Clear moon, frost soon.

*Michaelmas daisies take centre stage alongside berries and golden
leaves in this autumnal garland. Harvest time and falling leaves
are the subjects of this month's bands and border designs.*

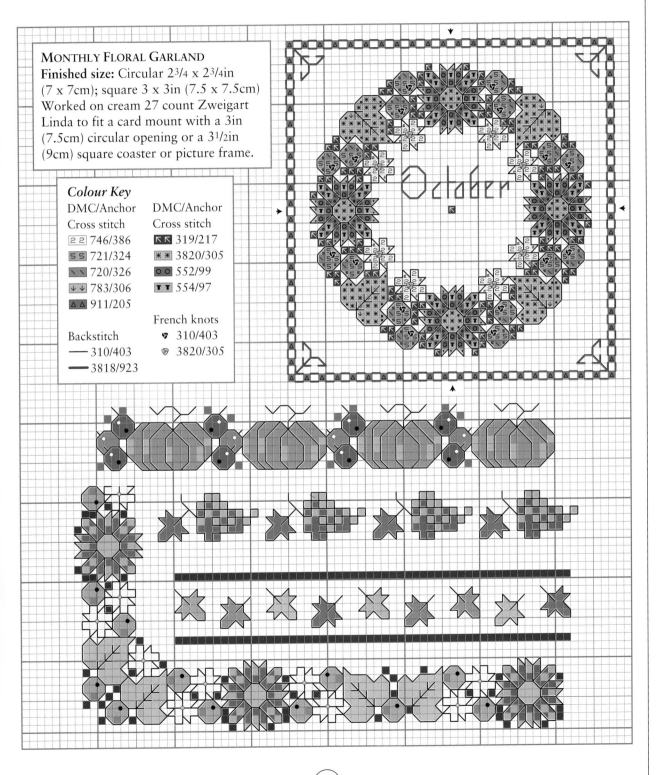

MONTHLY FLORAL GARLAND

Finished size: Circular 2³/4 x 2³/4in
(7 x 7cm); square 3 x 3in (7.5 x 7.5cm)
Worked on cream 27 count Zweigart
Linda to fit a card mount with a 3in
(7.5cm) circular opening or a 3¹/2in
(9cm) square coaster or picture frame.

Colour Key

DMC/Anchor	DMC/Anchor
Cross stitch	Cross stitch
2 2 746/386	↖ ↖ 319/217
5 5 721/324	＊ ＊ 3820/305
↘ ↘ 720/326	O O 552/99
↓ ↓ 783/306	T T 554/97
△ △ 911/205	

French knots
🌀 310/403
🌀 3820/305

Backstitch
—— 310/403
—— 3818/923

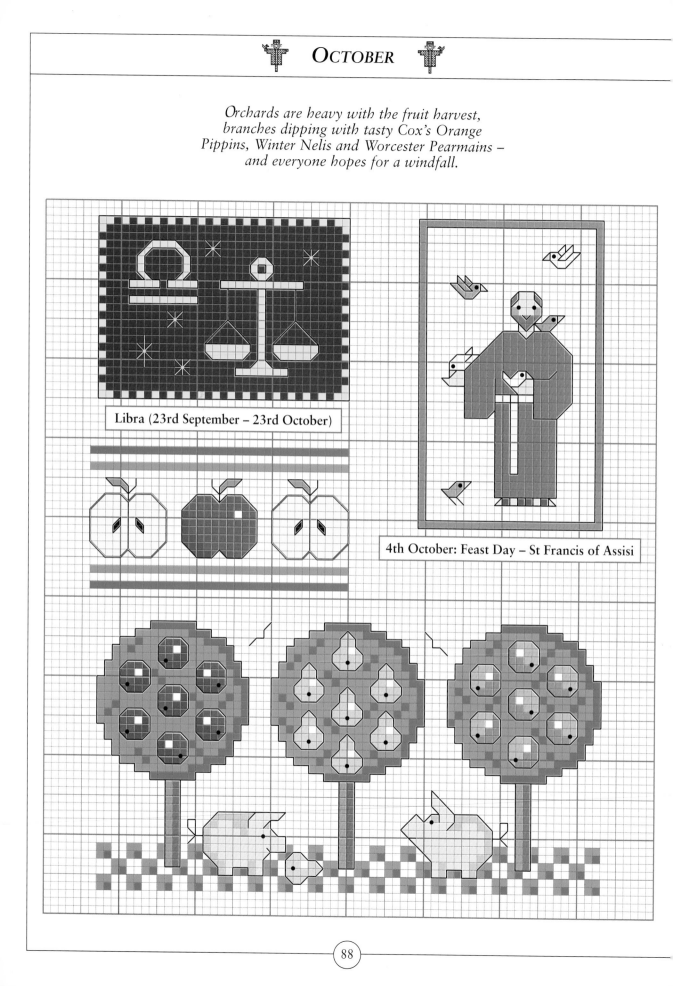

*Orchards are heavy with the fruit harvest,
branches dipping with tasty Cox's Orange
Pippins, Winter Nelis and Worcester Pearmains –
and everyone hopes for a windfall.*

Libra (23rd September – 23rd October)

4th October: Feast Day – St Francis of Assisi

October is a month of religious celebration for many around the world. During Diwali, the festival of light, Hindus hope that Lakshmi, the Hindu goddess of wealth, will visit and bless the house with good luck and a prosperous new year. The Jewish New Year festival, Rosh Hashanah, is also celebrated, and apples dipped in honey are eaten in the hope that the new year will be a sweet one.

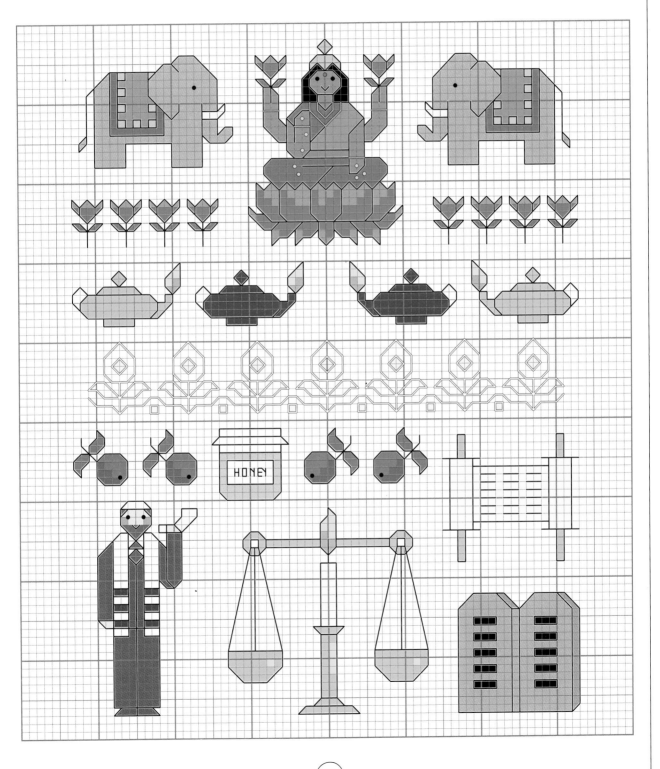

*In October beer festivals abound, including the world famous Munich Oktoberfest.
But there's no reason why wine-lovers shouldn't celebrate too.*

Hallowe'en gives children the chance to have some spooky fun. Choose from a wizard, witch, bat, mummy, Dracula, ghost, skeleton or Frankenstein's monster. Statutory toads and black cats complete the line-up.

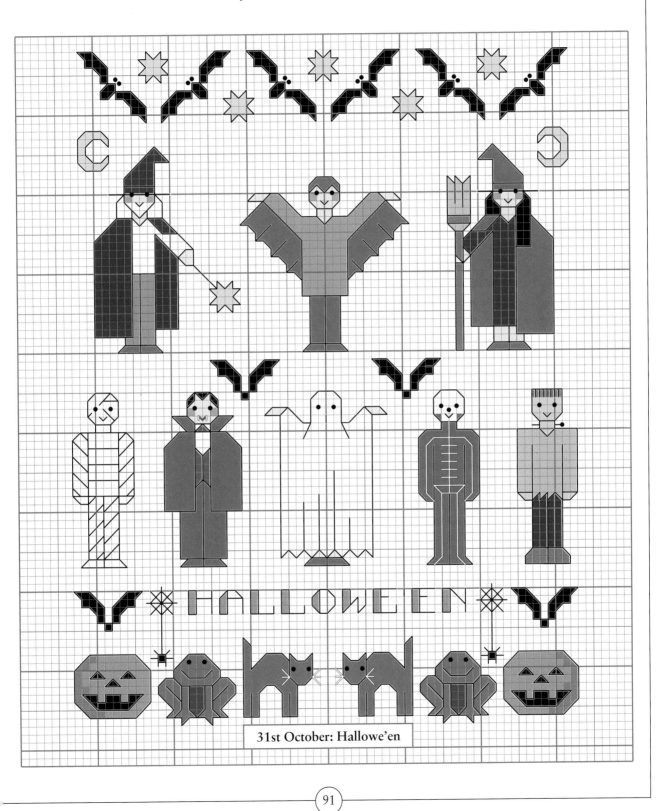

31st October: Hallowe'en

NOVEMBER

Ice in November to bear a duck,
The rest of the winter'll be slush and muck.

Hellebores, berries and ivy have been gathered together for November's birthday card garland. Beneath are other seasonal bands and a border.

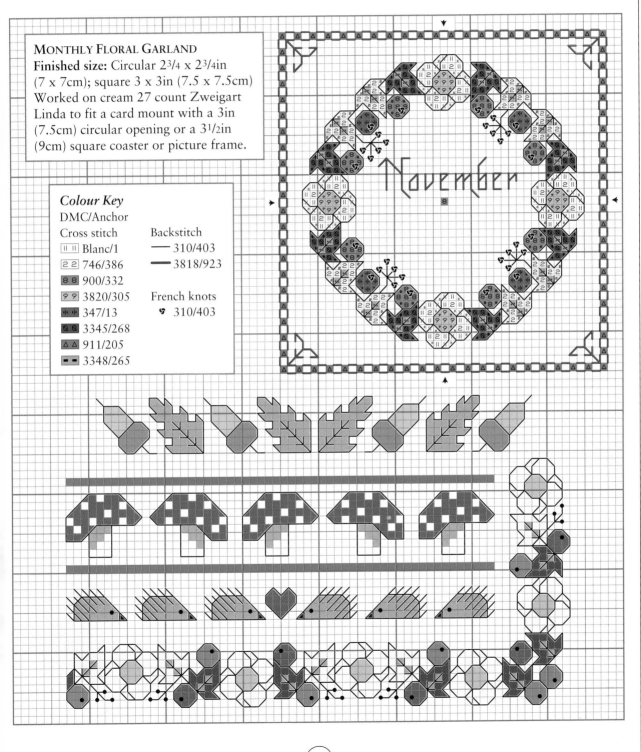

MONTHLY FLORAL GARLAND
Finished size: Circular 2³/4 x 2³/4in
(7 x 7cm); square 3 x 3in (7.5 x 7.5cm)
Worked on cream 27 count Zweigart
Linda to fit a card mount with a 3in
(7.5cm) circular opening or a 3¹/2in
(9cm) square coaster or picture frame.

Colour Key
DMC/Anchor
Cross stitch
⫼⫼ Blanc/1
22 746/386
88 900/332
99 3820/305
347/13
3345/268
△△ 911/205
3348/265

Backstitch
— 310/403
— 3818/923

French knots
♥ 310/403

Remembrance Day (Veteran's Day, USA) on the Sunday nearest 11th November, commemorates the anniversary of the armistice of World War I in 1918 and is observed to honour all (living or dead) who have served in the armed forces.

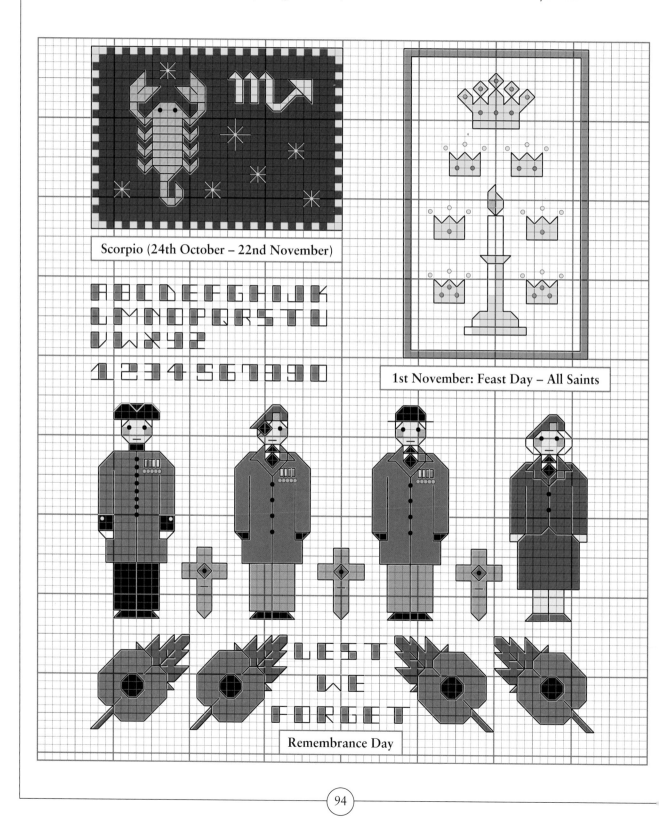

Scorpio (24th October – 22nd November)

1st November: Feast Day – All Saints

Remembrance Day

Other notable November dates to remember include St Andrew's Day, the patron saint of Scotland, and Thanksgiving Day, the fourth Thursday in the month, which commemorates the first successful harvest of the Plymouth colonists who shared a celebratory dinner of turkey and pumpkin pie with their Native American neighbours.

30th November: St Andrew's Day

Thanksgiving Day

November can be a very muddy month, so what do the men enjoy doing?
They play rugby. Scrums, tackles, tries and conversions are all in an afternoon's play.

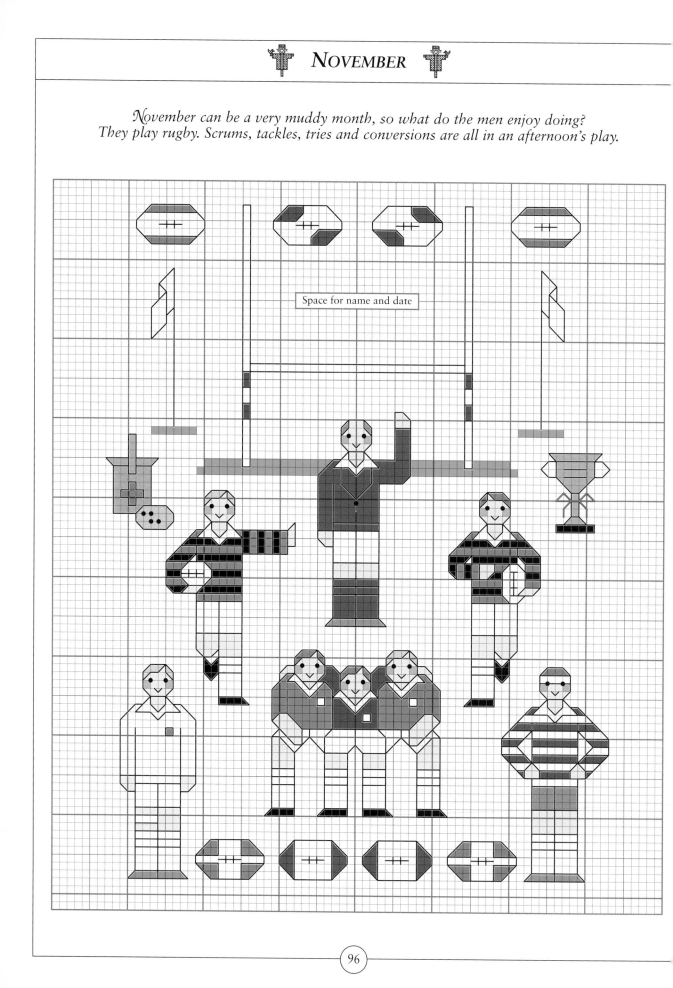

Space for name and date

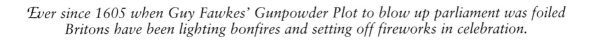

Ever since 1605 when Guy Fawkes' Gunpowder Plot to blow up parliament was foiled Britons have been lighting bonfires and setting off fireworks in celebration.

5th November: Bonfire Night

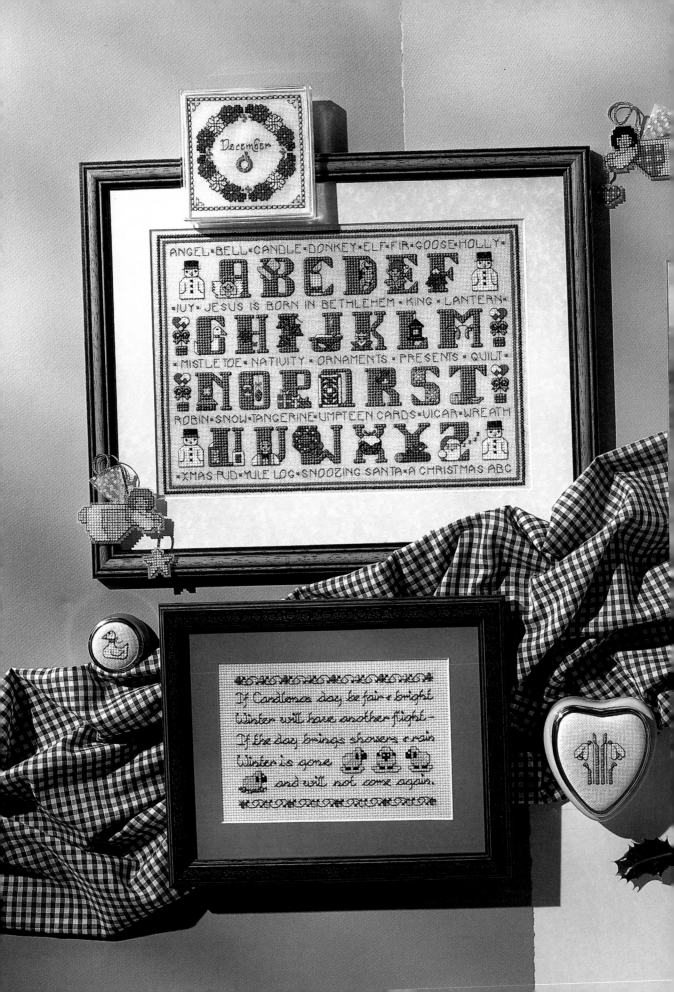

December

ANGEL ∗ BELL ∗ CANDLE ∗ DONKEY ∗ ELF ∗ FIR ∗ GOOSE ∗ HOLLY

A B C D E F

IVY ∗ JESUS IS BORN IN BETHLEHEM ∗ KING ∗ LANTERN

G H I J K L M

MISTLETOE ∗ NATIVITY ∗ ORNAMENTS ∗ PRESENTS ∗ QUILT

N O P Q R S T

ROBIN ∗ SNOW ∗ TANGERINE ∗ UMPTEEN CARDS ∗ VICAR ∗ WREATH

U V W X Y Z

XMAS PUD ∗ YULE LOG ∗ SNOOZING SANTA ∗ A CHRISTMAS ABC

If Candlemas day be fair & bright
Winter will have another flight –
If the day brings showers & rain
Winter is gone and will not come again.

WINTER

*H*olly berries shining red
*M*ean a long winter, 'tis said.

*Stitch-off-the-page designs
to celebrate the season of winter.*

WINTER ALPHABET
(charted on pages 100–101)
Finished size: 9³/4 x 7¹/4in (25 x 18.5cm).
Worked on cream 27 count Zweigart
Linda. Letters from the alphabet can be
extracted to stitch initials, names or events
through the season.

WINTER BAND SAMPLER
(charted on page 102)
Finished size: 3¹/2 x 9¹/2in (9 x 24cm).
Worked on 28 count Country Style
Evenweave (NJ449.11).
When work is complete, stitch a seasonal
brass charm onto the heart at the bottom of
the design. To prevent tarnishing, clean
brass charms with alcohol and seal them
with a thin coat of clear varnish before
applying them to embroidery. Frame the
sampler or hang it from bell-pull ends to
make a small hanging.

WINTER WEATHER FOLKLORE
(charted on page 103)
Finished size: 5¹/2 x 3³/4in (14 x 9.5cm).
Worked on cream 14 count Zweigart Aida.

THE GARDEN IN WINTER
(charted on page 104, photographed on page 105)
Finished size: 6 x 6³/4in (15 x 17cm).
Worked on 28 count Country Style
Evenweave (NJ449.11).

*Winter Alphabet, Winter Band Sampler and Winter Weather
Folklore, plus other items from this season. Each month also
has a photograph showing a variety of completed pieces to
give you some ideas on how the charts may be used*

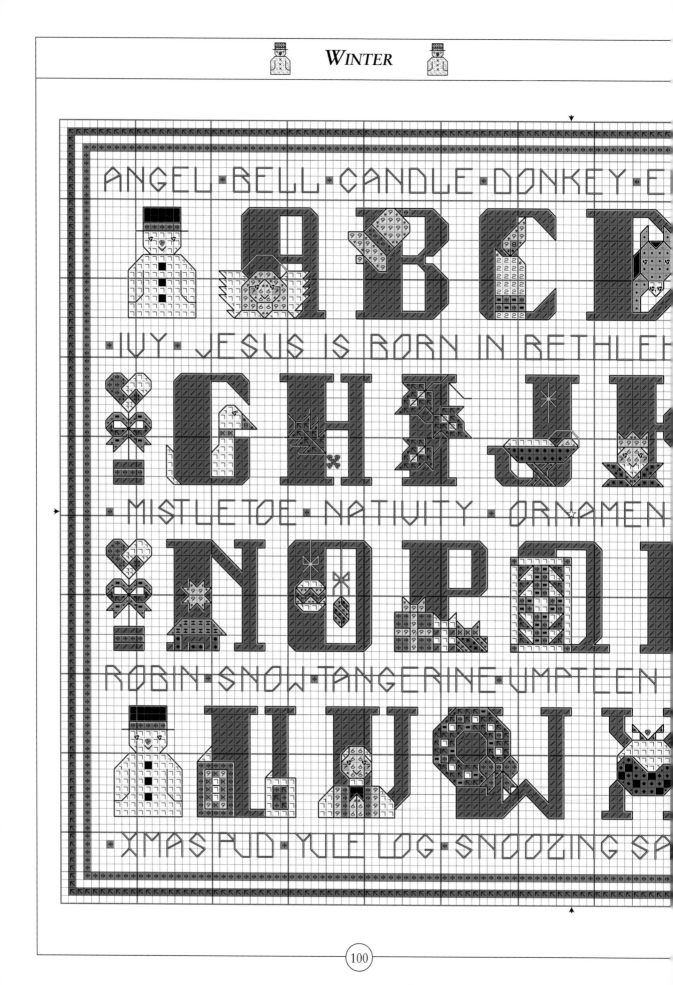

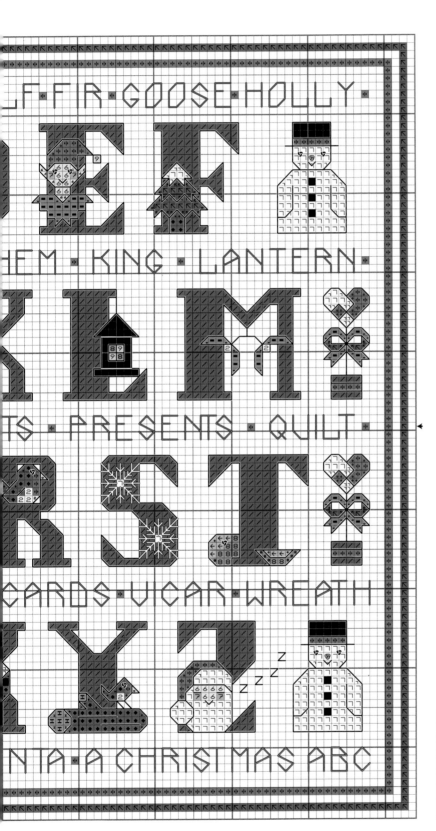

WINTER ALPHABET

Colour Key

DMC/Anchor
Cross stitch

• •	415/398
■	310/403
⊓ ⊓	Blanc/1
2 2	746/386
6 6	353/6
7 7	352/9
8 8	740/304
9 9	726/295
⟋⟋	701/227
K K	996/433
⊹⊹	321/9046
← ←	742/302
▬ ▬	703/239
⟋⟋	699/923
✱ ✱	552/99
◆ ◆	801/371
⌶ ⌶	435/369

Backstitch

——	310/403
——	321/9046
——	726/295
——	699/923
══	Blanc/1

French knots

❧	310/403
❧	740/304
❧	321/9046

☆ Middle point

Pale moon doth rain
Red moon doth blow
White moon doth neither
Rain nor snow.

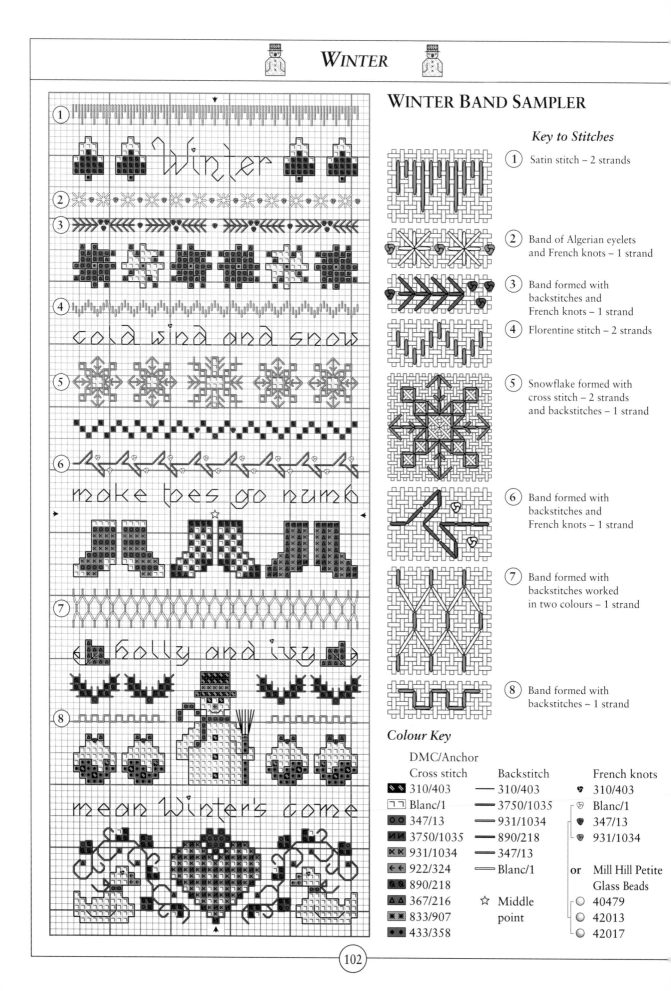

WINTER BAND SAMPLER

Key to Stitches

1. Satin stitch – 2 strands

2. Band of Algerian eyelets and French knots – 1 strand

3. Band formed with backstitches and French knots – 1 strand

4. Florentine stitch – 2 strands

5. Snowflake formed with cross stitch – 2 strands and backstitches – 1 strand

6. Band formed with backstitches and French knots – 1 strand

7. Band formed with backstitches worked in two colours – 1 strand

8. Band formed with backstitches – 1 strand

Colour Key

DMC/Anchor

Cross stitch	Backstitch	French knots
310/403	—— 310/403	310/403
Blanc/1	—— 3750/1035	Blanc/1
347/13	—— 931/1034	347/13
3750/1035	—— 890/218	931/1034
931/1034	—— 347/13	
922/324	—— Blanc/1	**or** Mill Hill Petite Glass Beads
890/218		40479
367/216	☆ Middle point	42013
833/907		42017
433/358		

> *If Candlemas day be fair & bright*
> *Winter will have another flight –*
> *If the day brings showers & rain*
> *Winter is gone and will not come again.*

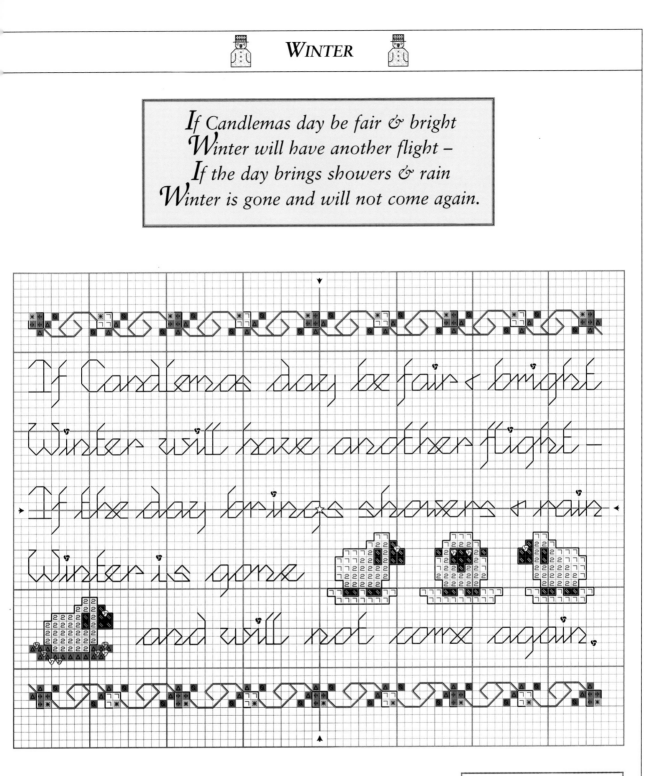

WINTER WEATHER FOLKLORE

2nd February: Candlemas

Colour Key
DMC/Anchor

Cross stitch			Backstitch	French knots	
310/403		304/47	—— 310/403	♥	310/403
Blanc/1		890/218	—— 890/218	♡	Blanc/1
367/216			☆ Middle point	♥	3821/306
3078/300		3821/306			

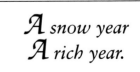

A snow year
A rich year.

THE GARDEN IN WINTER

Colour Key

DMC/Anchor

Cross stitch

·· 414/235	–⁄ 738/361	44 321/9046	99 699/923		Backstitch
					— 310/403
⁄⁄ 415/398	‖‖ 353/6	55 Blanc/1	00 720/324		— 720/324
⫿⫿ 701/227	‖‖ 352/9	66 301/349	×× 796/133		— 433/371
	22 798/131	77 307/289	∧∧ 809/129		— 701/227
	33 433/371	88 310/403	HH 316/1017		— Blanc/1

French knots
- � Blanc/1
- 🎗 310/403
- ◈ 699/923

☆ Middle point

DECEMBER

Christmastide comes in like a bride
With holly and ivy clad.

*It is all too easy to forget December birthdays in the rush to get ready for Christmas
but this garland of poinsettias and holly will ensure that nobody feels overlooked.
Seasonal bands and borders add a festive touch to your stitching.*

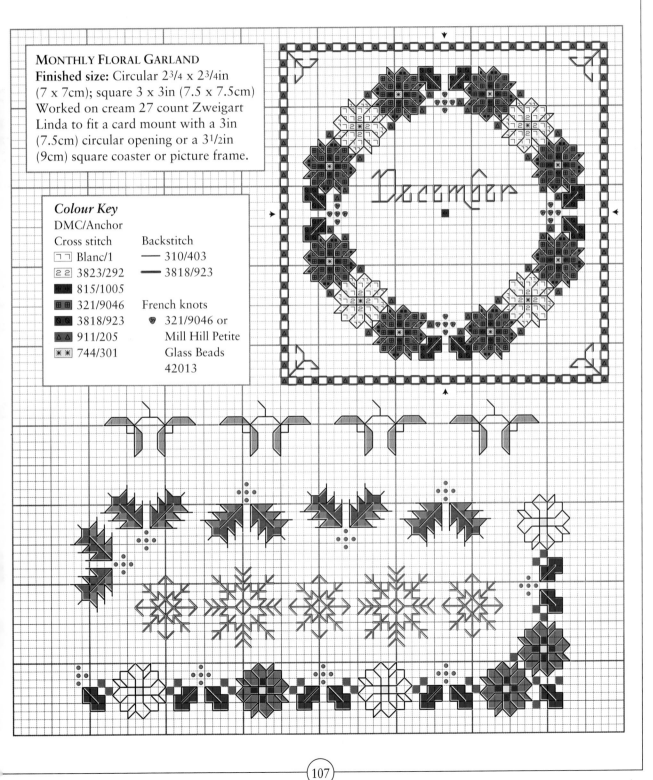

MONTHLY FLORAL GARLAND

Finished size: Circular 2³/4 x 2³/4in
(7 x 7cm); square 3 x 3in (7.5 x 7.5cm)
Worked on cream 27 count Zweigart
Linda to fit a card mount with a 3in
(7.5cm) circular opening or a 3¹/2in
(9cm) square coaster or picture frame.

Colour Key

DMC/Anchor

Cross stitch	Backstitch
꺾꺾 Blanc/1	— 310/403
2 2 3823/292	— 3818/923
▦▦ 815/1005	
⊞⊞ 321/9046	French knots
◙◙ 3818/923	♥ 321/9046 or
△△ 911/205	Mill Hill Petite
✷✷ 744/301	Glass Beads
	42013

Behind every successful Christmas lies an exhausted mother, but sitting down to stitch the three small cards below and opposite is my recommended therapy.

Sagittarius (23rd November – 21st December)

25th December: Feast Day – Christmas

These Christmas angels with their stars and hearts are quick to make when time is short. You can hang them as a festive mobile or on the branches of the Christmas tree, changing the colours to complement your decorative theme. For stitching and making up instructions turn to page 126.

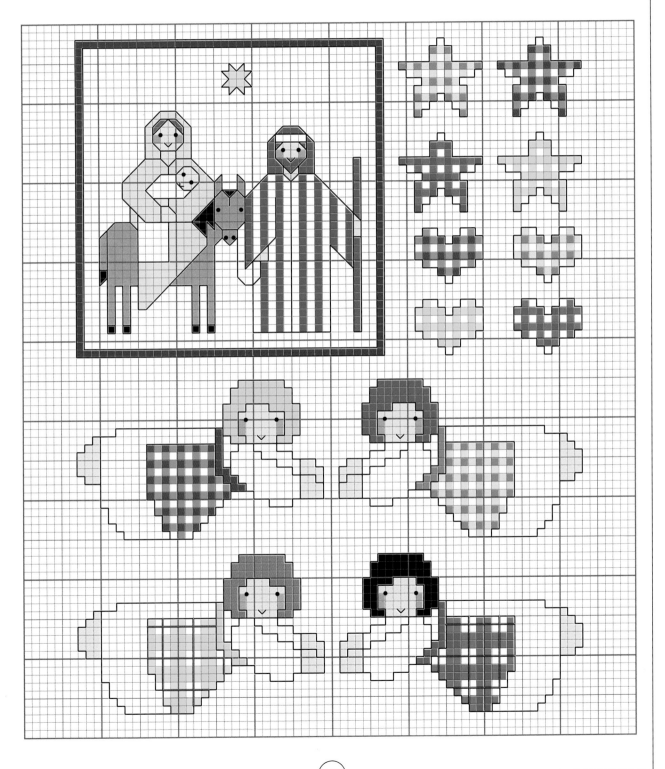

The Twelve Days of Christmas.
Is it really only twelve days?
It seems to go on for a lot longer in my household.

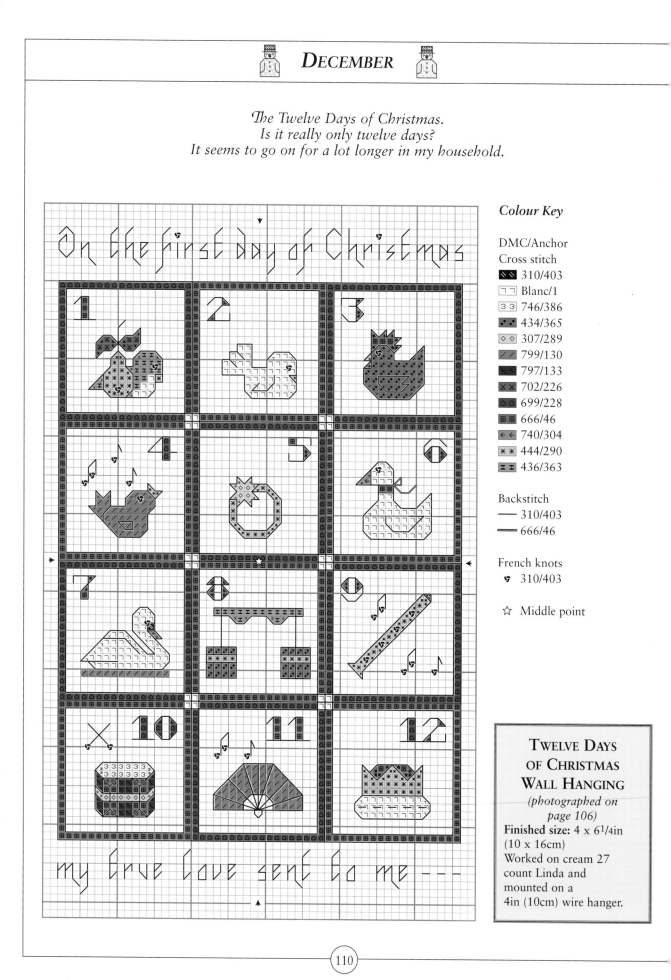

Colour Key

DMC/Anchor
Cross stitch
310/403
Blanc/1
746/386
434/365
307/289
799/130
797/133
702/226
699/228
666/46
740/304
444/290
436/363

Backstitch
—— 310/403
—— 666/46

French knots
310/403

☆ Middle point

TWELVE DAYS OF CHRISTMAS WALL HANGING
(photographed on page 106)
Finished size: 4 x 6¹/₄in (10 x 16cm)
Worked on cream 27 count Linda and mounted on a 4in (10cm) wire hanger.

When cold weather keeps most of us huddled by the fire, keen types can take their pick of the winter sports: from curling to ice hockey, skiing to skating, or simply tobogganing and having snowball fights, participation will get the blood coursing.

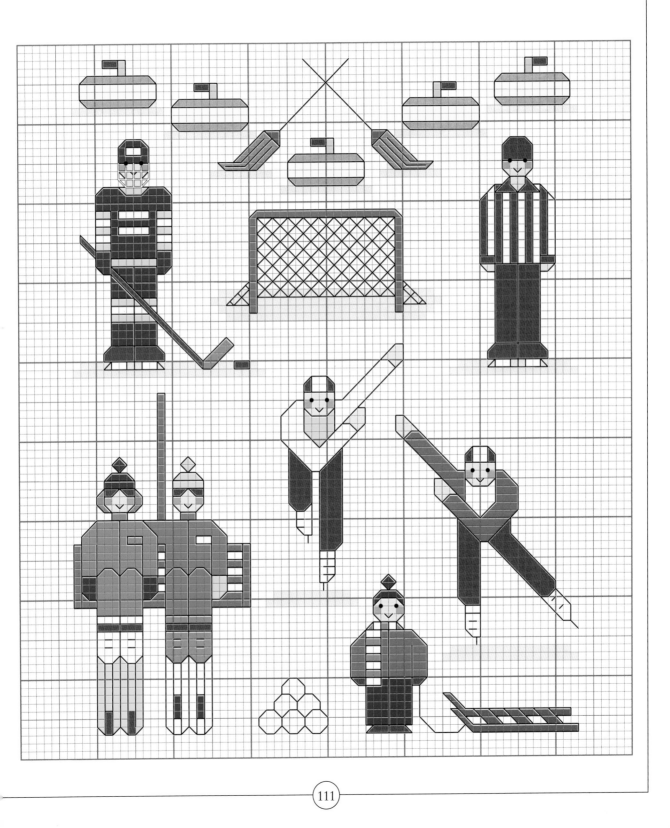

JANUARY

Yule is come, and Yule is gone, and we have feasted well;
Now Jack must to his flail again, and Jenny to her wheel.

Winter aconites brighten up grey January days and have been chosen for this month's birthday garland. Indoors, potted cyclamens bring a splash of colour to our homes.

MONTHLY FLORAL GARLAND
Finished size: Circular 2³/₄ x 2³/₄in
(7 x 7cm); square 3 x 3in (7.5 x 7.5cm)
Worked on cream 27 count Zweigart
Linda to fit a card mount with a 3in
(7.5cm) circular opening or a 3¹/₂in
(9cm) square coaster or picture frame.

Colour Key
DMC/Anchor

Cross stitch	Backstitch
Blanc/1	— 310/403
307/289	— 3818/923
911/205	
563/208	French knots
704/238	307/289
444/291	

*Supporters of American Football eagerly await the Super Bowl, the
annual championship game of the National Football League
in the USA which takes place on the last Sunday in January.*

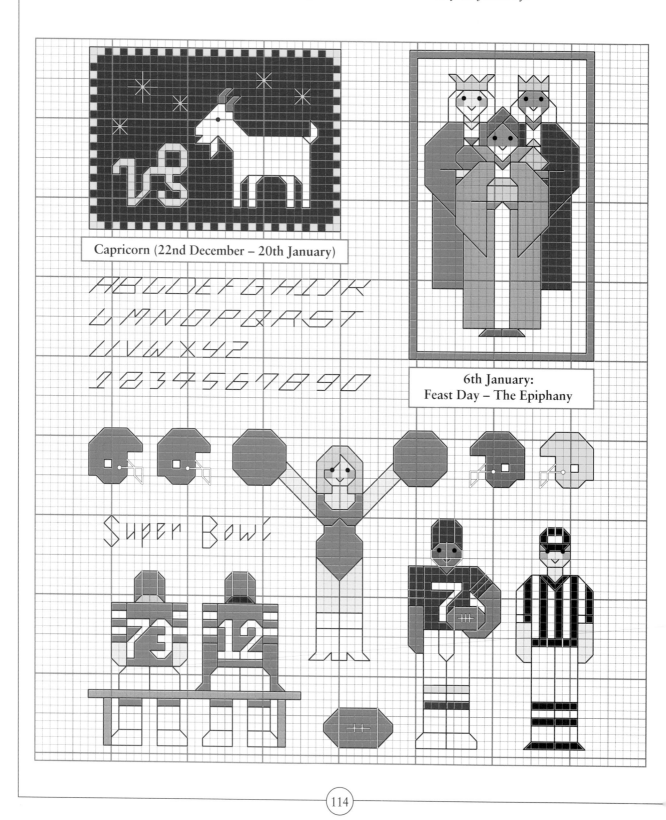

Capricorn (22nd December – 20th January)

6th January:
Feast Day – The Epiphany

We bring in the New Year by linking hands and singing For Auld Lang's Syne at the last stroke of midnight. After a night of revelry it may be time to make some sober New Year resolutions.

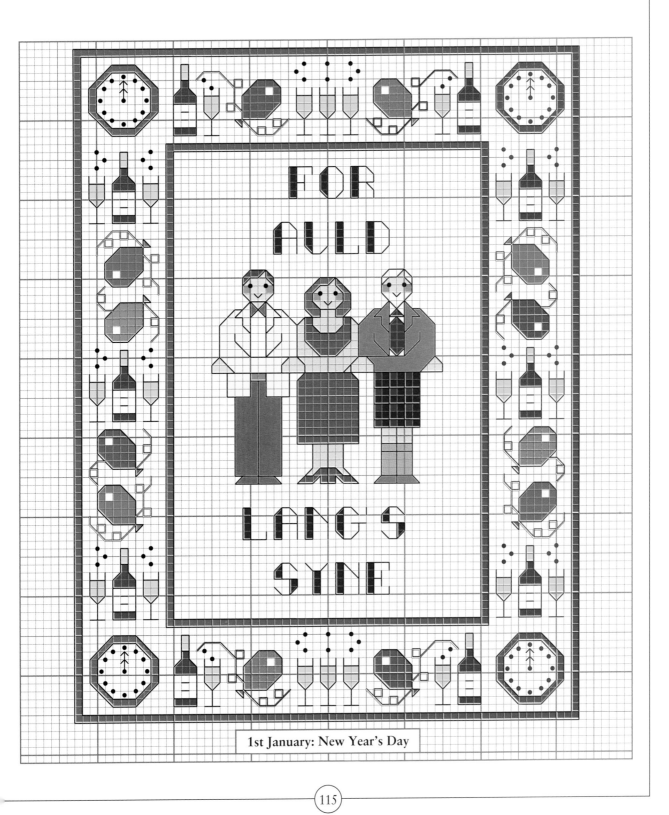

1st January: New Year's Day

Men dress up as women, girls dress up as boys –
it must be the pantomime season again.

Cinderella, Aladdin, Puss in Boots, the fairy godmother and Dick Whittington and his cat all make an appearance, along with my favourites – the pantomime cow and horse.

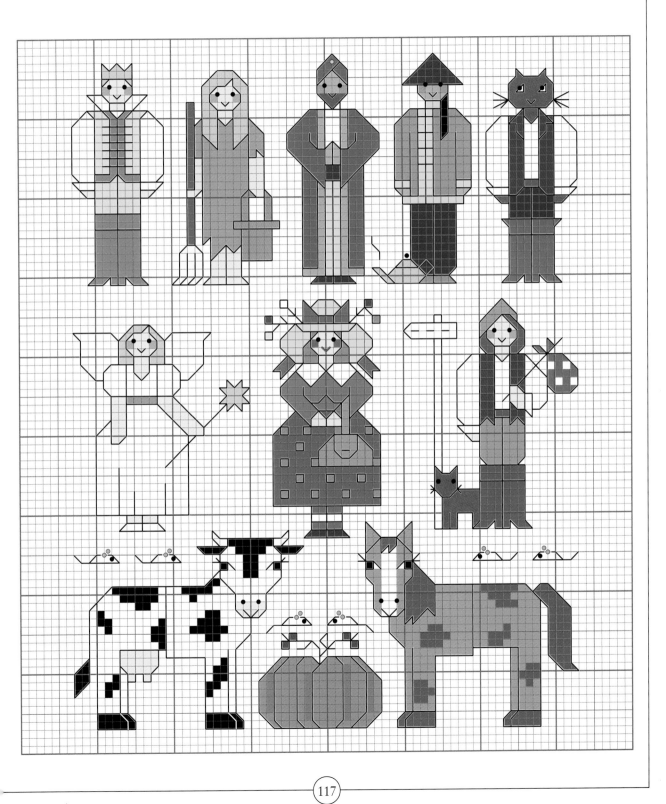

FEBRUARY

All the months in the year curse a fair February.

Snowdrops and crocuses give the first hint that spring is on the way and how glad we are to see them appear. A circle of crocuses forms a garland for the February birthday card, whilst snowdrops nod and irises bloom below.

MONTHLY FLORAL GARLAND
Finished size: Circular 2³/4 x 2³/4in
(7 x 7cm); square 3 x 3in (7.5 x 7.5cm)
Worked on cream 27 count Zweigart
Linda to fit a card mount with a 3in
(7.5cm) circular opening or a 3¹/2in
(9cm) square coaster or picture frame.

Colour Key
DMC/Anchor

Cross stitch	Backstitch
Blanc/1	310/403
742/302	740/304
743/301	3818/923
911/205	742/302
340/118	

*Love is in the air, doves are cooing and birds are beginning
to nest and feed their young.*

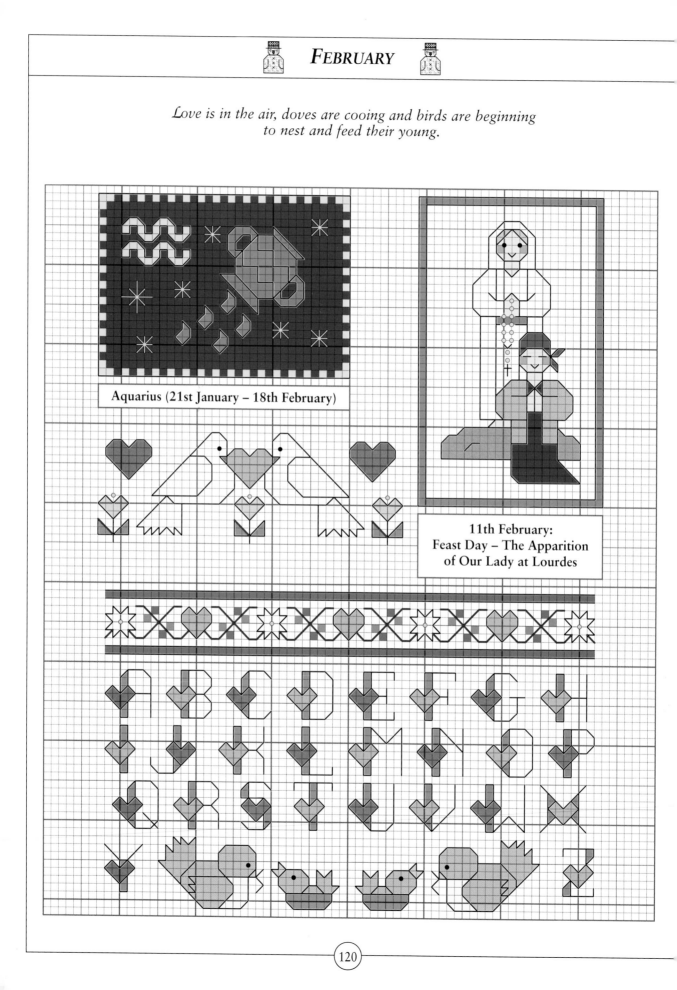

Aquarius (21st January – 18th February)

11th February:
Feast Day – The Apparition
of Our Lady at Lourdes

Valentine's Day gives us the opportunity to show our appreciation of our chosen partner with a romantic card or gift. Husbands should note that diamonds are most acceptable.

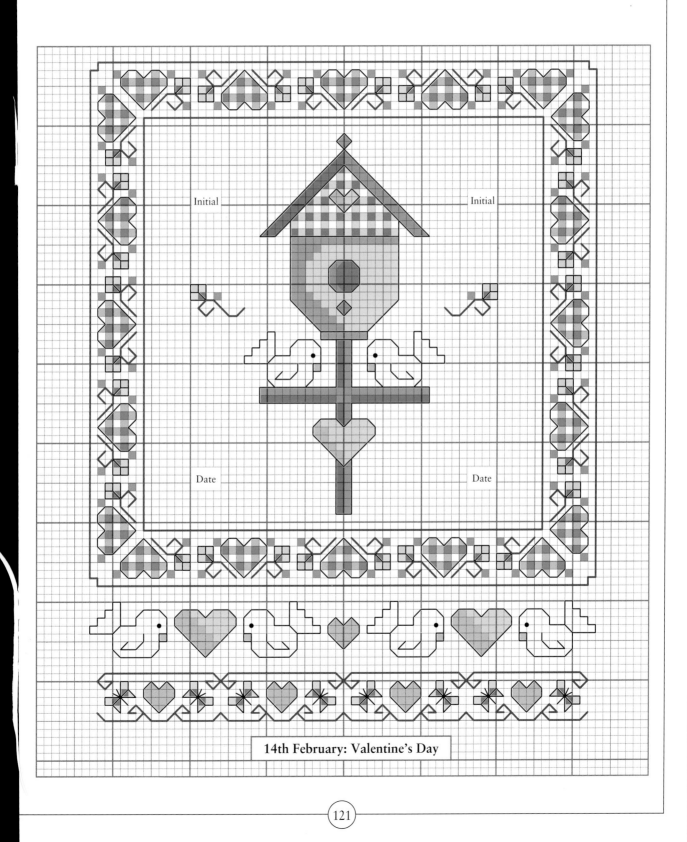

Initial

Initial

Date

Date

14th February: Valentine's Day

February may be the shortest month, but it is full of days to remember. President's Day (USA) falls on the third Monday in February and honours George Washington and Abraham Lincoln. Shrove Tuesday (Pancake Day) heralds the beginning of Lent in the Christian calendar. During a Leap Year (on 29th February) you can ask the man of your dreams to marry you.

Chinese New Year. Years in China are named after twelve animals which have been used in strict rotation since the sixth century. Each animal is said to have its own characteristics which are found in people born that year. For example, 1998 is the Year of the Tiger and courage is a characteristic attributed to Tiger Year people; 1999 is the Year of the Rabbit; the year 2000 is the Year of the Dragon and so on. Read the chart from top left to bottom right, line by line, to calculate which animal rules the year in which you were born.

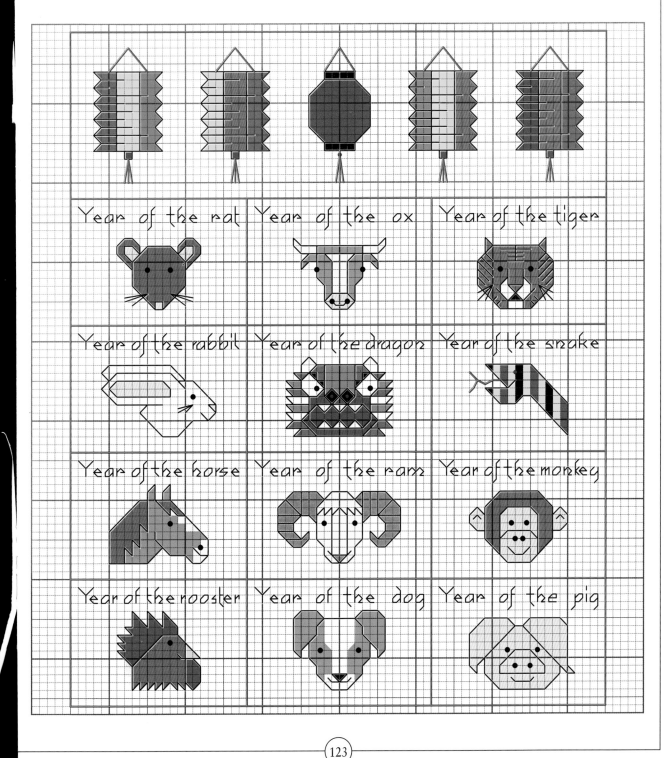

MOUNTING EMBROIDERY INTO A CARD

A ready-made mount has three sections and an opening already cut in it (see Figs 24 and 25). Establish which is the top and which is the bottom of the card. The border at the top of a card is generally narrower than the border at the bottom.

1 Lay your embroidery on section (b) and trim the embroidery so that it is ¹⁄₂in (1.5cm) larger than the opening.

2 On the inside of the card, stick strips of double-sided sticky tape around the opening and on section (a) as shown in Figs 24 and 25. The shaded area on section (a) indicates a squirt of aerosol adhesive such as Spray Mount. This is sprayed on to give the embroidery a sticky surface to cling to as without it the embroidery has a tendency to ripple. Place the card in an up-turned cardboard box, with the inside facing you. Cover sections (b) and (c) with a piece of scrap paper. Apply the aerosol adhesive to section (a). The box and scrap paper will stop the adhesive going where it is not wanted.

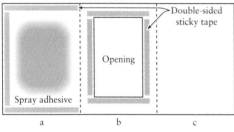

Fig 24 Mounting into a card with
a rectangular or square opening

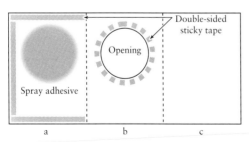

Fig 25 Mounting into a card with
a circular or oval opening

3 Next lay your embroidery face up on a flat surface. Remove the backing strips from the sticky tape on the card. With the outside of the card facing you, stick the opening around your embroidery, making sure that it is centred and straight. Do not worry if you do not get it right the first time as the double-sided tape will allow you to make several attempts. Fold section (a) over section (b), stroke down firmly and write your message on section (c). Add any trimmings required.

COVERING A PHOTOGRAPH ALBUM

To cover a photograph album, first make sure that you have chosen a suitable album. Some flip-up albums are not suitable for this treatment, as the fabric pockets prevent the photographs from flipping up.

1 Fold your chosen fabric around your album, then cut enough fabric to allow for turnings and two end pockets. Tack the fold lines and make a note of which section is to be embroidered (Fig 26).

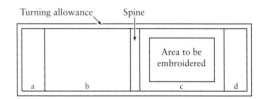

Fig 26 Layout of fabric to be cut for a
photograph album cover (right side)

2 If your album has a dark-coloured cover that will show though the embroidery fabric, lining is recommended. To do this, tack a similar sized piece of white cotton fabric to the back of your embroidery fabric when stitching is complete.

3 Hemstitch the turnings on the inside of the cover. With wrong sides together, fold section (a) over section (b) and slipstitch as shown, to form a pocket. Repeat with the other end, fold section (d) over section (c) and slipstitch to form another pocket (Fig 27). Remove all tacking thread. Slip the album cover into the two end pockets and smooth the cover into place.

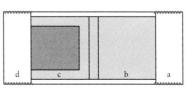

Fig 27 The finished cover (wrong side)

MAKING A BAND

There are many Aida bands available that are suitable for designs which contain only full cross stitches, but for designs which contain three-quarter stitch it is best to work on evenweave fabric.

1 Embroider your band then neaten the raw edges and hem them on the back of the work. Disguise the hem line with braid, ribbon or lace.

2 Stitch strips of white Velcro to the ends of the band so that it can be removed for laundering.

A simple band can be constructed by stitching embroidery firmly to decorative ribbon. Cover the raw edges of the embroidery with decorative braid, or remove a few threads of the embroidery fabric for a fringed effect.

MAKING A WALL HANGING

The size of fabric you cut will depend on your fabric and bell-pull ends. Allow enough fabric on either side of the embroidery and at the top and bottom for turnings.

1 When stitching is complete, fold the work in half lengthways with right sides together and stitch a seam down the side (Fig 28). Turn right side out so that the seam is at the centre back, then press carefully.

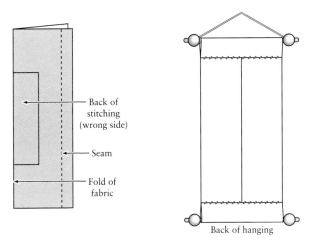

Fig 28 Making a wall hanging (wrong side)

2 Neaten the top and bottom, fold 1in (2.5cm) over the top bell-pull end and slipstitch into place at the back of the work. Repeat with the bottom of the hanging. Cover any traces of slipstitching with decorative braid if necessary.

MAKING A BIBLE MARKER

Finished size of embroidery: 1³/4 x 3in (4.5 x 7.5cm). Worked on white 27 count Zweigart Linda. In order not to damage the fine pages of a Bible, only one single thickness of ribbon should be allowed to lie between the pages. The embroidery therefore should be applied to the ribbon and should hang below the pages. You will need a length of satin 70mm ribbon.

1 Fold the ribbon in half, right sides together and seam from (a) to (b) to make the pointed end of the marker (Fig 29). Turn right side out.

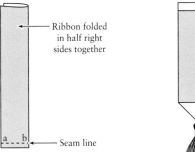

Fig 29 Seaming ribbon to make a pointed end on a bible marker

Fig 30 Finished marker (wrong side)

2 Turn the top of the ribbon over ¹/2in (1.5cm) and then again another ¹/2in (1.5cm). Use Wundaweb bonding fleece to hold the hem in place so that no stitching is visible on the front of the ribbon.

3 Trim the embroidery four threads from the edge of the stitching. Stitch it to the ribbon with tiny invisible backstitches as close to the embroidery as possible. Remove the threads up to the stitching line for a fringed effect or cover the raw edges with a fine gold braid.

4 Attach a tassel as shown in Fig 30. To make a tassel, cut two rectangular pieces of card the same size. The length will be determined by the size of the card. Lay a loose thread between the two pieces of card; this will be used to attach the tassel to the ribbon. Wrap thread around the pieces of card until there is sufficient on the card to make a tassel of the thickness you require (Fig 31 overleaf). Tie a knot in the loose length of thread to hold the tassel together at (a). Slip your scissors between the two pieces of card and cut through the loops at (b). Tie a short length of thread firmly around the tassel at (c) (Fig 32).

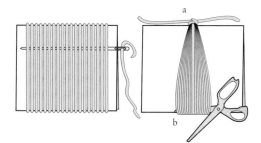

Fig 31 Wrap thread around the pieces of card to the thickness you require the tassel

Fig 32 Tie a short length of thread firmly around the tassel

MAKING THE ANGEL CHRISTMAS TREE HANGINGS
Finished size: 2¹/2 x 1¹/2in (6 x 4cm)
1 Use 14 count plastic canvas or Vinylweave and the chart on page 109. When work is complete, cut out the angel leaving one free strand of the canvas all around.

2 To make the wings, cut a 2¹/2in (6cm) semicircle of net. Fold the semicircle in half and then in half again. Stitch the wing to the angel's back.

3 Cut a loop of fine gold cord for a hanger and stitch this to the angel's back just behind her head. Cut out a stitched star or heart and hang it from the angel's hand using fine gold cord.

4 Back the angel and the star or heart with white 14 count Aida or Christmas fabric glued into place to hide the back of the embroidery.

FRAMING
Any embroidery that is to be placed in a frame is best taken to a reputable framer as a good framer will give your work the professional finishing touch it deserves. Ask to have the work mounted onto acid-free card to avoid unsightly brown spots (foxing) which can develop later. All my framed work is finished with clear glass that is not allowed to come into contact with the stitches, to avoid flattening them. This is achieved by using an acid-free mount, or by placing fine strips of acid-free card around the edges where the overlap of the frame will hide them from view. To prevent fading, avoid hanging your embroidery in full sunlight.

When mounting work into purchased items such as porcelain bowls, key tags, credit card holders etc, follow the manufacturer's instructions. Where it is necessary to cut the fabric close to the embroidery, first back it with iron-on Vilene to stabilise it and prevent fraying.

ACKNOWLEDGEMENTS

Without my team of dedicated needlewomen who helped me with the stitching of samples and who gave so generously of their time, this book would not have seen the light of day before the millennium. A huge thank you therefore to, Win Barry (April, May, June floral garlands), Gill Broad (Thanksgiving, pigs in orchard), Audrey Bryan (Calendar of Feast Days), Carol Burr (The Garden in Summer), Eileen Callender (June wedding and accessories), Hazel Evans (January, February, March floral garlands), Ros Foster (photo album cover, Sowing Peas), Margaret Jones (Valentine and teacher pictures, Bethlehem card, zodiac key tag, tulip credit card holder, compact mirror, My Kitchen), Sandra Kedzlie (Easter, Jo's kitchen fridge magnet, Fall, Noel), Elizabeth Lovesey (Easter bible marker, Christmas porcelain bowls, gardener's card, Remembrance Day poppy, teacher's pencil pot, thistle storage box, piper notebook, kitchen card), Edna McCready (The Twelve Days of Christmas), Sue Moir (Winter Alphabet, May Day), Sue Moore (The Garden in Autumn,

Cinderella), Sylvia Morgan (Spring Alphabet, mother pig), Val Morgan (Spring, Summer, Autumn and Winter Band Samplers, Christmas angels, mother hen), Penny Peberdy (Autumn Alphabet), Jenny Potts (Spring, Summer, Autumn and Winter Weather Folklore), Amanda Salethorn (sunflower band, New Year band, snowdrop bowl), Ann Sansom (Summer Alphabet, Superbowl mug, Golden Glow card), Linda Smith (The Garden in Spring), Nancy Verso (August and September floral garlands, Hallowe'en card, Chinese New Year), Irene Vincent (The Garden in Winter, sporting clock, Up the Rovers!), Jenny Way (October, November, December floral garlands). Between us we produced 97 pieces of stitching in all.

Many thanks also to Cheryl Brown, Brenda Morrison, Kay Ball and Lin Clements at David & Charles for all their hard work and encouragement, to Ethan Danielson who made sense of the charts and never once shouted at me and to David and Kit Johnson for the delicious photographs.

When contacting suppliers through the post for catalogues or other information,
please always enclose a stamped-addressed envelope. If you telephone them they
will be able to tell you if there is a charge for their catalogue or price list.

I am indebted to the following suppliers for their most generous assistance in the production of this book:

Cara Ackerman at: DMC Creative World
Ltd, Pullman Road, Wigston,
Leicestershire LE8 2DY.
Tel: (01162) 811040.
*(Zweigart fabrics – Linda, Aida, Rustico,
Brittney, DMC stranded cottons, DMC
seed beads, card mounts.)*

Alastair McMinn at: Coats Patons Crafts,
McMullen Road, Darlington, Co Durham
DL1 1YQ.
Tel: (01325) 381010.
(Anchor stranded cottons, Offray embroidery ribbon.)

Mike Gray at: Framecraft Miniatures Ltd,
372-376 Summer Lane, Hockley,
Birmingham B19 3QA.
Tel: (0121) 2120551.
Mail order service and list of overseas
suppliers available.
*(Baby booties, Fun Clips for welly pegs,
compact mirror, credit card holders, key
tags, storage box, pencil pot, notebook,
fridge magnet, wooden bell-pull ends,
porcelain and wooden bowls, ring box,
place cards, black cat, turkey, pumpkin,
watermelon and flowerpot buttons,
Vinylweave, Mill Hill Petite Glass Beads,
football card mount)*

Voirrey Branthwaite at: The Voirrey
Embroidery Centre, Brimstage Hall,
Wirral, L63 6JA.
Tel: (0151) 3423514.
Mail order service available.
*(14 count plastic canvas, 28 count Country
Style Evenweave fabrics.)*

Len Turner at: Fabric Flair, Unit 3,
Northlands Industrial Estate, Copheap
Lane, Warminster, BA12 0BG.
Tel: free phone (0800) 716851.
(Jobelan fabrics, coaster.)

Sue Rhodes at: Bead Exclusive, 4 Samara
Park, Cavalier Road, Heathfield, Newton
Abbot, Devon TQ12 6TR.
Tel: (01626) 834934.
(Bunny beads in April mini-display case.)

Paul and Jacqui Smith at: Hantex Ltd,
Unit 8-9 Lodge Farm Business Units,
Wolverton Road, Castlethorpe, Milton
Keynes MK19 7ES.
Tel: (01908) 511428 for information
pack and stockists.
*(Brass charms for floral garlands and
band samplers, novelty buttons – harvest
moon, vase, bucket, rolling pin, fruit,
pencil, ruler, pencil sharpener, Americana
4th July, Trena's Trinkets seed packet and
bee buttons, heart-shaped wire hanger.)*

David Macleod at: Macleod Craft
Marketing, West Yonderton, Warlock Road,
Bridge of Weir, Renfrewshire PA11 3SR.
Tel: (01505) 612618.
(Super Bowl Stitch-a-mug.)

Phil Jackson at: Beamers, School House,
Westhope, Herefordshire HR4 8BU.
Tel: (01432) 830466.
(Chicken picture frame, flower box picture frame.)

Jenny Kearley at: Craft Creations Ltd, 1B
Ingersoll House, Delamare Road,
Cheshunt, Herts EN8 9ND.
Tel: Enquiries (01992) 781900;
Catalogues only (01992) 781903.
*(Greetings card mounts, tracing graph
paper.)*

Tara Hobson at: Card Shop (code:
QAE/30/CS), Future Publishing Ltd,
Somerton, Somerset TA11 6TB.
Tel: (01458) 271138.
*(Gardeners, kitchen, and Golden Glow
card mounts.)*

John Evans at: The Sewing Basket Card
Co, 14 Kensington Industrial Estate, Hall
Street, Southport, Merseyside PR9 0NY.
Tel: (01704) 536040.
(Greetings card mounts.)

Impress Blank Cards and Craft Materials,
Slough Farm, Westhall, Halesworth,
Suffolk IP19 8RN.
Tel: (01986) 781422.
(Bethlehem card mount.)

Ian and Martin Lawson-Smith at: IL-Soft,
5, 6 & 7 Spinners Court, West End,
Witney, Oxon OX8 6NJ.
Tel: (01993) 779274.
*(Cross Stitch Designer Gold: Premium
Plus computer software, together with
much help and support.)*

Allan Suttie at: Fastframe, 5 Church
Street, Rugby, Warks CV21 3PH.
Tel: (01788) 542713.
(Framing.)

Boots the Chemists, with stores nation-
wide, provided the easel-shaped frame
(Page 80).

My local branch of Hobbycraft Art &
Craft Superstores, Tyne Road, Weedon
Road Industrial Estate, Northampton
NN5 5AF.
Tel: (01604) 591800 (personal shoppers
only).
*(Provided the 4th July vine wreath, clock
frame and movement, mini-display cases,
sun hat, bible book-mark ribbon and
many of the miniatures and small items
which appear on these pages.)*

INDEX